INHERITING THE HOLOCAUST

INHERITING THE HOLOCAUST

A Second-Generation Memoir

Paula S. Fass

RUTGERS UNIVERSITY PRESS
NEW BRUNSWICK, NEW JERSEY, AND LONDON

Library of Congress Cataloging-in-Publication Data

Fass, Paula S.
  Inheriting the Holocaust : a second-generation memoir / Paula S. Fass.
    p. cm.
  Includes bibliographical references and index.
  ISBN 978-0-8135-4458-8 (hardcover : alk. paper)
  1. Jews—Poland—Lódz—History—20th century.   2. Holocaust, Jewish
(1939–1945)—Poland—Lódz—Personal narratives.   3. Holocaust, Jewish
(1939–1945)—Influence.   4. Fass, Paula S.—Travel—Poland.   5. Children of
Holocaust survivors—Biography. I. Title.
  DS134.62.F37 2009
  940.53'18092—dc22
  [B]   2008013960

Frontispiece: Paula Fass and her mother, 1949

A British Cataloging-in-Publication record for this book is available from the British
Library.

Visit our Web site: http://rutgerspress.rutgers.edu

Manufactured in the United States of America

For my children,
Bluma Jessica Lesch and Charles Harry Taylor Lesch

and

In memory of my parents,
Bluma Sieradzka Fass and Chaim Harry Fass

The evil day has arrived.
The evil hour has arrived.
When I must teach you, a little girl,
The terrible parsha of *Lekh Lekho*.

—*Simchar Bunim Shayevitsch*
written in the Lodz Ghetto

CONTENTS

ACKNOWLEDGMENTS

Almost a decade ago, during a long conversation with Berel Lang at Trinity College, I expressed my fears about writing about the Holocaust. The book became a possibility when he assured me that I would not be exploiting but giving shape to a sacred memory. An unusual excursion in 2001 with Linda Kerber and Stanley Katz, hosted by Douglas Greenberg to the Shoah Foundation for Visual History in Los Angeles gave me a much-needed push. Some of the most difficult writing took place in Valauris, France, where my good friend Lois Champy opened her beautiful home to me and my daughter in May and June 2001. I am very grateful for her hospitality. I am also grateful for the warm welcome extended to me and my husband Jack by Elzbieta and Wiesiek Oleksy in Lodz, Poland, and for Michael Thaler's kindness when he and I were both in Lodz in May 2000. Mateusz Oleksy was an excellent guide to Lodz Province in 2007. James Sheean gave me a serious historical podium from which to make my memories into history at the American Historical Association in January 2006.

Over the years of its composition, various colleagues and friends have read versions of this book and provided moral support and encouragement. Many of them also provided important suggestions. I want to thank Robert Middlekauff, Mary Ann Mason, Deborah Gershenowitz, Kendra Boileau, Bluma Lesch, and Ira Lapidus. Gerry Caspary was a guiding light, taking time from his own memoir to offer many excellent readings and sensitive suggestions. To my sorrow, Gerry died during its production. During an academic leave in 2006–2007 spent at the Center for Advanced Study in the Behavioral Sciences at Stanford, funded by the Guggenheim Memorial Foundation, I was able to finish the revisions. At the center, I had the good fortune to make friends with Dolores Hayden and Peter Marris, both talented writers and extraordinary people. Each gave me invaluable advice, and I will always remember Peter's enormous kindness and brilliant reading. I am deeply saddened that he died before its publication. At Rutgers University Press, the manuscript has been shepherded through the production process with devoted attention by Leslie Mitchner, Allyson Fields, Lisa Jerry, Alison Hack, and Alicia Nadkarni. I am extremely grateful to them for their care and hard work.

My daughter, Bibi, and my son, Charles, have been constant inspirations as well as companions in my search for meaning. Jack Lesch, my life partner and best friend, has been my polestar since my mother died and left the memories to me.

INHERITING THE
HOLOCAUST

INTRODUCTION

INHERITING MEMORY

I am the daughter of Holocaust survivors. This fact has been inscribed in my identity since I was a child in postwar Germany, and almost all of my memories of that time are related to it. But my life has not been devoted to exploring this part of my past. Although I have spent my professional life studying history, only recently have I drawn this unique personal past into the spaces of what I call history.

Most of my life I kept my personal past and the historical past separated. Nineteen years ago, I chaired the plenary session of the 1989 meeting of the Organization of American Historians. The session about history and memory included a large number of prominent American historians who spoke about their own memories of World War II. I did not speak. I, born amidst its ruins, was the product of that war; my parents were among the very small remnant of the Jewish community of Poland who had survived Auschwitz and other camps. But my memories I then believed could not be included. Because I was born after the war my memories did not count. They were secondhand memories, inadequate to the task of reconstructing history. I was a responsible historian, and therefore I did not, could not, speak of my experiences of World War II.

In this book, I have decided to speak and to share my memories because I now firmly believe that my memories do count. Certain memories are so profound, so much part of the bone and marrow that they are inheritable. Inherited memories of this kind have meaning and importance for historians. In the last twenty years, a variety of organizations have been devoted to collecting the testimony of survivors of the Holocaust and preserving the memories of those who, like my parents, witnessed both the life and the death of a culture and the people who created and sustained it. They had been witnesses to a barbarous destruction. And historians assume the task of documenting the life, and, in some terrible cases, the death of societies and cultures,

Neither of my parents lived to become resources for this crucial historical project. My mother, who died thirty years ago, had an extraordinary memory, detailed and vivid, and her stories of life as a young woman in the Jewish Poland of the 1920s and as a young wife and mother in the 1930s were deeply ingrained in my childhood and youth. So were her much more troubling recollections of the Lodz ghetto, Auschwitz, and Bergen-Belsen. Immediately after her liberation my mother had the number she was given in Auschwitz (BK 8589) inscribed on a silver coin (inside of a Star of David). This was a memory she needed to preserve.

My father had his own engraved memories, though he shared these far less often with me. His were memories of a mature businessman who traveled through Poland looking to make a living while he raised a family. He never discussed his four children with me; these children and his wife were exterminated sometime between January 1943 and the fall of 1944. He was a very atypical survivor, a man in his forties when he was finally liberated alone from the deadly Ahlem labor camp. He died more than twenty years ago.

Even at quite a young age I became a repository of these and many other facts, as my mother passed on to me stories she wanted me to know. These are the memories I have now come to share as a daughter and as a historian. Indeed, I cannot remember a time when I did not know that my mother and my father were survivors. In my home this meant only one thing—they had escaped Hitler's deadly curse upon the

Jews. They had survived, but hardly fully in either body or spirit. Even a child could see and understand that. And they had left behind in this hellish past everyone who had mattered to them—brothers and sisters, mothers and fathers, husband and wife, uncles, aunts, cousins, friends, and children.

Although many of their memories became mine, it was always clear to me that the loss they had experienced would never be mine. Because I had not suffered, I imagined that the memories themselves were not really mine or rather that I had no claim to them because my memories lacked the pain that was theirs. If I had not suffered, then I had no authentic memories. It has taken me many years to recognize that not only are the memories mine but that some of the pain is mine as well.

For most of my adult life as a professional historian, I have considered the social dimensions of human experience, but only in relation to others, mostly anonymous others, who became the subjects of my historical reconstruction. I have been concerned with how personal identities are created, how human bonds are defined, and, most recently, with the loss of those bonds. During most of my life as a professional historian, my parents' lives and their experience were bracketed. Although these have always been the source of my engagement with the past as a very real place, I considered them and their experience unique. Hitler set them (and me) apart in a bubble, and we and a small community of those like us had been left to drift into the modern world. History was about the lives of other people, the kind of people I had made it my task to know as a professional historian. These people's experiences or identities somehow intersected with my own, but they were people whose histories I did not share. Although others around me began to explore what came to be called the Holocaust as a monumental historical event, I set myself the task of writing the history of the people whose lives I shared in the present, not in the past. Like Ruth, I chose that these adopted people would become my people as I followed the land of my arrival rather than the place of my departure. I have never regretted the choice.

Now, I have come to reclaim this other history, the history that my parents gave me in the form of memory. I am convinced that this memory is essential so that the experience of the Holocaust can be fully known and documented. Only memory can make the astounding magnitude of Holocaust destruction into real history; only memory can prevent its reduction to the incantation of a bewildering number whose dimensions are just too huge to be humanly meaningful. I hope the following demonstrates that even the memoir of a single family can reveal the richness and diversity of the people erased by the Holocaust. Only a wide range of witnesses to the past can give texture and historical depth to a diverse people. Because my parents died too long ago to participate in recent projects that seek out survivors, my memory will have to provide the materials they can no longer recount; I must preserve those remnants and shreds of memory from the dwindling reservoir of the human experiences of those people and those times. Thus, I hope that I can contribute to the necessary historical reconstruction of the lives of Holocaust victims and the few survivors, a project that both confirms the enormity of the catastrophe of the Shoah and creates a more specific picture of human loss. This remembrance adds to the mountains of the dead a more robust knowledge about the living and a more enduring sense of the meaning of the extermination. I hope that I can count myself among those historians, not because I was trained in Eastern European history or the history of the Shoah, but because as the daughter of survivors and the sister of the dead, I know many things about them that we need to preserve. Thus my memories, memories of memories, secondhand goods, but of vintage quality, are necessary parts of that history and of the resources historians can use. This much I have learned during the last nineteen years.

The following memoir is neither a substitute for the large and important historical literature on the Shoah nor the personal record of a survivor. Like all children of survivors, even those who were told a great deal, details, facts, and circumstances are missing from the stories I was told and the memories shared with me. In trying to reconstruct specific events and the lives of the lost, I often have nothing more than a few bare details, details that I have refused to embellish even with the historical imagination that I have developed as an adult. Instead, I have tried to gather my memories about the lives of all those meaningful people whom my parents knew and about a way of life of which my parents were deprived when they became survivors. To this I have added some of my attempts to find these people in the very few records that remain. In what follows, it is the lives of these people I am hoping to recover, although their deaths intrude on all sides. So necessarily does my own life and experience, not only because finally my memories and not theirs are the subject of this book but also because as a child of survivors and as a historian I write with a sense of how my personal life and my subsequent career were shaped by the people whose lives were dominated by an immense historical event to which I have become a reluctant witness. Whereas histories try to reconstruct large views of the lived experience of the past, memoirs can only contribute small splinters to that reconstruction. These splinters provide each of us with a personal past and allow our memories to become part of what constitutes the history we pass forward.

As the daughter of a specific family, I do not claim to speak for all children of Holocaust survivors, but I imagine that what I have to say will resonate with the experiences of others and encourage them to think of themselves as part of a historical generation, singed by the conflagration at the center of the twentieth century which destroyed their families' Europe and forced them to become engaged in the creation of a new postwar world. Their history and my history are important because we were at once part of the abomination of the Holocaust but have been rescued into a much better life. This is something I did not understand most of my life. As the children of survivors, we knew how beastly life and the men and women who created it could be. But our own lives were also blessings and reprieves from that history. That confusing knowledge,

which was nothing like survivor's guilt but engaged some of its terrible
ambiguity, made our childhoods, our educations, and our mature lives
unique and historically important.

In the following memoir of my family, I embrace both the memories
bequeathed to me by those who survived and my memories of a very
specific kind of childhood that resulted in the adult I became. I am very
much aware of the difficulties that memories present to the historian, of
their testy trustworthiness. But memories, just like all historical sources
require elaborate scrutiny. I have found that my memories proved good
enough to recover the documentation of two families who were formed
in Lodz between two world wars and managed to live in the beastliness of the Litzmannstadt ghetto for four years. My memories were
good enough to find the names of lost children and even cousins who
were never mentioned by name, good enough to reconstruct streets and
neighborhoods in a city whose name had reverberated throughout my
childhood but which I visited only in middle age, good enough, in fact,
not to be entirely discarded as we seek to reconstruct the plenitude of
Jewish life in European culture before the great destruction. Such memories are not easily forgotten.

CHAPTER 1

GOING TO POLAND

MAY 2000

When I was a child, I thought there was no reason to ever go to Poland except for the diamonds. In one of his rare loquacious moods, my father told me that he had buried a large can containing diamonds deep in the ground in the Lodz ghetto. He had transformed all his money into diamonds to preserve it. It would enable him to start up again after the war. I wanted him to go back to reclaim his fortune. My sister and I even told him that we would go instead, if he would only tell us where to look. "No," he said very deliberately and with a short laugh. "I will never go back to Poland. And you would be wasting your time. The authorities would never just let you dig around in the ground. Besides, a large post-war building or other structure now surely sits on the site." My father added, "It was not diamonds that I left behind."

My father hated Poland. He had no positive feelings about either the nation or its people. He even hated his memories of Poland. He was a Jew. While we, in the United States, might today say that he was a Polish Jew, his Polish identity meant little to him, and it could hardly describe his relationship with a nation that came into existence two decades after he was born and then disappeared when Hitler occupied the western half of the country and incorporated Lodz, my father's birthplace, into the German Reich. For almost two centuries, Poland was real only in people's minds. And my father was not one of those people who kept Poland in his mind. He would never have called himself a Polish Jew. When asked where he was from, he always said that he was "from Lodz." My father and his family became occupants of a small part of Polish history by some demonic fate, but neither he nor they were Polish. Poland represented nothing much to him except another form of oppression and Jew hatred. He never spoke Polish fluently and did not read or write Polish. He had gone to a Polish secular school only briefly. He became literate in Yiddish, which he learned at a Jewish *heder* (Hebrew school), much as generations of his male ancestors in most parts of Europe had done for centuries; there he learned to read and write.

When I decided it was time to begin to understand my other history, the history I had not learned at school, by traveling to Poland, the decision was somewhat strange. In my own mind, because I had begun my American history by voyaging as a child to a new world, I sought to reverse the process, reappropriating a place and a past I had largely ignored as a child when I told people that I was born in Germany while making it clear that I was not German. In the past, when I traveled to "Europe," with which I identified (though not to Germany), I had fooled myself into believing that I was going back home, searching everywhere I could for the differences I had come to recognize from my mother's description of her past and her home. I sought outdoor markets and large, dark, quaint furnishings, fresh local foods, inner courtyards and ancient water pumps. I had convinced myself these were European, but I had never dreamed of going to Poland.

I went to Poland in the new millennium because the stories my mother told me about her past were almost all located there. My mother's feelings about Poland were more complex than my father's. She told me many stories about anti-Semitism that included ugly acts of hostility, such as the time that a couple of Polish youths cut off my grandfather's *pais* (side-locks). They solidified this humiliation by calling him a dirty Jew (*Zyd*). Still, she was proud that she spoke an urbane and well-inflected Polish (rare among survivors), and she taught me about

Copernicus, Chopin, and Marie Curie with pride. Poland, I learned from her, had good reasons to see itself as a proud European nation that had made significant contributions to European culture. She had no doubt learned both the language and the pride in *Polonia* in school. Unlike my father, she had once had Polish friends since she had grown up in a mixed Polish-Jewish neighborhood, yet she also had no interest in ever going back to Poland. I would go in their stead, after my parents had died to look for their past in a society that neither had loved.

I always feel some anxiety before going on a trip, a combination of concerns about flying and the pain/excitement of leaving home. But my anxieties before leaving for Poland on May 9, 2000, were of a different order entirely. In addition to flying and separation fears, I feared both what I would find and what I wouldn't find. I went to modern Poland— postwar, postcommunist, post-Warsaw Pact—to seek a Poland once inhabited by my parents, a Poland from which they had been extruded in a process that combined absolute personal humiliation and a tenuous march toward death. I was going to this Poland, which for them was at once a place of nostalgic youth and beastly memory, to find what?

I told myself that, as a historian, I now sought a far more personal history than the history about which I wrote and taught. I wanted to give this history to my children, American born and bred, in order to leave them some shreds of a past that had always been my intimate companion in the memories my mother shared with me and the knowledge of life my father had tried to impart. I also sought to preserve knowledge about their past as part of what I was beginning to understand as my obligation as a historian with certain kinds of connections to memory. This past and these people once quite familiar to me as a child, were altogether foreign to my children, though they knew of course that my parents were Holocaust survivors and I an immigrant to this country. This past had increasingly become foreign to me as well because I had been separating myself from it as I grew to become American. Now, I wanted it back. Growing older had made me realize that the professional history with which I had surrounded myself as an adult had left a small emptiness of self and a larger emptiness of connection that I owed to myself as well as to my parents. I also needed deeply to make the connection between this past and my children. Erik Erikson had called this drive for connection "generativity" and described it as a sign of healthy development as we get older. I thought of it in very personal terms. I wanted to tell my children about people they had not known (my parents) and about people even I had not know (my grandparents, uncles, aunts, cousins, brothers and sisters). I needed to leave some documentation of the lives my parents could no longer tell about but whose importance they imparted to me as an inheritance. I thus hoped to create some history from the shreds of memory that remained in me. This repossession of a personal past required that I go to Poland, not because it was beloved by either my parents or me, but because it was where they had started. It was the place where their past, of which I had only my memories of their memories, had taken place. These memories I now sought to repossess.

Personal memory I knew to be an imperfect historical source, an untrustworthy connection. Still, I now sought it hungrily, despite its slippery hold on reliability. When I was very young my mother had told me that when she was liberated from Bergen-Belsen, where she had served as spokesperson among a group of survivors, she had proposed that they give up their personal lives, put on long drab robes, and go about the country telling their story, that they dedicate their lives to the telling. Immediately after the war, she who had arrived in Auschwitz "too late" to have the blue number imprinted onto her arm, had it inscribed into the first coin she ever received. Later I learned to call this "bearing witness," making concrete that which is personally fleeting, by carving it into social space. It is neither how she finally lived out her life, nor is it a path I chose for my own. It had taken me a long time to realize that what she had instinctively sought to do was what I as a historian had been training to do. With time, I had trained my voice by degrees with my books and archives so that I could finally hope to have the skills and the courage to write something for my own children and for anyone else who would listen, a history about a past and a people who would otherwise be altogether forgotten. I could not bear witness, but I could do as my mother had done, recount the experience of their lives and almost deaths, and inscribe some remembrance of those whose death had been so final that I hardly knew their names.

That history had taken place in Poland so I decided to go to Poland, where three and one-half million Jews lived just before the war and where my family had lived for generations before the war—first in Congress Poland, then in Russian-controlled Poland, and then in the Polish Republic, and finally, much more briefly, in the Poland absorbed into Hitler's Reich. In Poland they had lived and died. In Poland the luxurious growth of generations from both sides of my family had flourished and finally been destroyed. And it was from Poland that my parents had been driven out.

I would return with my fears and with my daughter. I brought her as a witness to my experience in the present (herself a fine keeper of journals), as emotional ballast, and as a means to make the generational connection firm. I was going back to try to coax memory forward so that the link between my mother's memories and my daughter's history could be made. My daughter, named for my mother, was a connection on the chain of generations and on the gossamer links of memory. The trip was also a personal vindication, a means to demonstrate that we had survived to reproduce and to return. At my worst moments, however, I feared that Poland would not release us, keeping for itself the very last remnant of my family, and we would be trapped in the cavern of the past that I had come to explore. More than once I held Bibi tight as I feared for our lives, hers and mine, as my mind slipped in confusion between the present in which we were just tourists in modern Poland and the past we had come to find.

Instead, we returned together to the United States, which had nourished me and borne her, just like most other tourists, full of the pleasures of traveling in contemporary Poland. I also brought back documents and renewed thoughts about the Polish past and a revitalized ability to remember. I returned from Lodz and Krakow, from Chelmno and War- saw, from Auschwitz and Birkenau with a real, though fleeting, sense of connection. On our voyage home we had stopped in Germany (a plane stop only), much as my parents had stopped in Germany (long enough for me to be born) in different circumstances and during an altogether other time. Half a century had turned out to be a very long time. We stopped at a modern airport in Munich, the city where my parents' near destruction had begun and which now had an excellent duty-free shop. One final time, as we were asked to give Lufthansa information about next of kin (to be notified, just in case), the apprehension of danger went through my head and through Bibi's as well, and it passed between our eyes. But it was just a passing glance as we bought chocolates and cognac and cosmetics in Munich.

The problem with the past is that it is always viewed through the present. That problem was intensified for me. I had returned to Poland as a historian to recover my family's experience and to refresh personal memories of that experience. Trying to bear a secondhand witness, I was confronted with the sharp edges of historical reality. As we tried to glimpse the past in modern Poland, it was now a country remade without Jews. Maybe that is why my parents never wanted to return.

———

Arriving in Warsaw at the beginning of the new millennium was a sober- ing experience. Greeted by a small and dingy airport where I waited for a long time at the carousel only to discover that the airline had lost my suitcase, I was soon confronted by taxi drivers desperate to earn some money and take tourists for whatever they could manage to extract. The city itself is large and grey. Most of historic Warsaw had literally disappeared, as the Nazis fanatically demolished the city by seeking to obliterate its independent past and its possible future. After the war, the

Poles had frantically tried to reclaim the capital; they rebuilt the city and reconstructed the Old Town in a Disneyland effort at historical verisimilitude. There are historical statues throughout the city, especially to Polish literary heroes, and at its center a beautifully restored park and garden has trees older than the nation itself. But almost nothing remains of the old Jewish ghetto, except for a segment of one street. The space once occupied by the ghetto and by its million people has been grandly commemorated with an enormous monument, the front of which shows in high relief the heroic resistance of the Polish people; the back depicts the beaten down shades of the obliterated Jewish ghetto uprising. The restored old synagogue is unused. At the center of Warsaw today, the tourist cannot avoid seeing the looming tower of communist culture constructed in the days of Soviet dominance. In front of my center city hotel Polish soldiers commemorated Józef Pilsudski's birthday. Pilsudski, the hero of Poland's reborn nationality after the First World War, is remembered today in a once again reborn Poland. Warsaw struggles to define its past, while it sheds its oppressors and reclaims its role as the capital of Polish nationality.

Warsaw meant little to me personally. My parents never spoke about the city except in the reverent tones of outsiders who knew about the city's size and importance. If they had ever visited, they did not tell me about it; they would have been tourists like me, except without the resources I could command to go to the best restaurants and shops. Because the airline had lost my suitcase, I had to seek out stores immediately where I could find basics, and Bibi and I spent the first afternoon scouting stores. The goods were unexceptional and mostly drab. Luckily, my suitcase was returned to me the next day.

Because Warsaw, in which I was purely a modern day tourist, was so lacking in appeal, I could creep gradually toward a much more familiar Poland. This happened on my third and last day in Warsaw, when I bought two combs in a department store and realized that I could make out the conversations taking place around me, conversations about

clothes, family, and the weather. I was startled and told Bibi with gushing
excitement that I could understand Polish. Poland had suddenly become
more than a tourist location. Being in Poland had opened a channel for
memory and personal experience. If this had happened in unfamiliar,
modern Warsaw, I began to anticipate far more as our sights turned
elsewhere. In the end, as a historical tourist, Poland provided me what I
would later describe to everyone, as an amazing experience. It gave me a
context to remember what I once knew and to imagine what I never had.
Poland gave me the opportunity to touch the past through language,
memory, and documents (the talisman of a good historian). It forced me
to confront contradictions in my emotions, in the country from which
my family came, and between the documents and my memories, contradictions that fed my sense of how truly amazing history is and how
profound the task of reconstruction.

Before leaving in May, I had been frequently told that anti-Semitism
was as rampant in Poland today as it had been in the past. Scolded by
some for going to a place where "they" hated us so much, I was asked
why I should support that country, its people, and that hatred? The
memories of my parents' stories about the deep-seated hatred of Jews
in Poland were always with me. The official attitude in Poland today is
a respectful sense of a once-important Jewish past conveyed by docents
and ordinary people who cluster around the killing grounds of places
like Auschwitz or Chelmno. It is also conveyed by the polite and helpful
Polish administrators at the Lodz ghetto archives and the participants at
the Yiddish theatre in Warsaw, none of whom speak Yiddish or understand it as natives. Over the course of two weeks, Bibi and I visited all of
these places and found people paying respectful homage to a past that
is now a source of historical reflection for those willing to reflect. There
are also swastikas on the walls, but people explained that these were
aimed, not at Jews, but at losing soccer teams. If there is anti-Semitism,
and I must believe those who know contemporary Polish politics far
better than I do and can penetrate the culture with greater sensitivity,

then it is mostly hidden and residual, no longer a fact of daily life. It is not obviously available to historical tourists. As the painful consciousness of anti-Semitism is awakened by historical narratives such as Jan Gross's accounts of wartime Jedwabne and postwar pogroms, these do, of course, also become current events. But, in the absence of a large Jewish community, it is an anti-Semitism of association rather than of active participation today.

In the Polish past, however, anti-Semitism was ubiquitous, as omnipresent as the churches and the discriminatory legislation, and the visible differences in the appearance of most Jews, like my grandfather with his beard and side-locks. Anti-Semitism existed in the separation between Jewish and Christian parts of small towns and larger cities, where Jews were usually a sizable minority (often 20 to 30 percent), and in the different lives these people lived. At the higher reaches of society, Jewish intellectuals and manufacturers were able to fashion lives among Poles and more fully integrate into Poland, but among the masses the two groups lived largely separate lives. This past can only be glimpsed by a historical tourist like myself, in the many churches that still function and the remnants of monuments to ghettos that no longer exist. It can also be glimpsed in the carefully reconstructed exhibitions in the shells of synagogues, such as those in Krakow that are nothing more than museums today.

Starting in Warsaw, I looked often into the faces of the passersby, hoping to find Jews and fearing to find the hatred of Jews. I do not know if I found either, because I could not tell. I saw many faces that looked like people I knew as my father's friends when I was a child. Were they Jews, or the descendents of Jews, maybe hidden Jews? Or was I just not sufficiently sensitized to locating those ineffable differences that someone like my mother claimed she could always spot. Maybe the Jews, far more than I was ever told, were more bound to the local Polish population, bound in blood as well as birth. They had been there for centuries, a part of Poland in almost all parts of Poland. My mother had assured me that she could always recognize a Jewish person in Poland; they were always distinguishable. But I could not recognize them today. Some had, after all, been hidden even during the worst of times, and some seemed to be there among the city's people, looking for all the world, like my uncle's friend, Mr. Goldberg, of the twinkling blue eyes. Maybe I was mistaken; maybe it was the way they wore their clothes or the way they walked, so unlike Americans, that reminded me of my parents' friends. But, even so, that meant that the Jews of Poland had somehow absorbed what the Poles have even today, the special appearance of the country of their birth. Even Mr. Nitsky, with whom as a teenager I argued about Jewish orthodoxy, looked in his stature, in the way he wore his hair and in his coloring, like the Polish men I saw in Warsaw.

There are very few Jews in Poland today except in the cemeteries, and even the cemeteries do not contain all the Jews of Polish history. I went to three of these—in Warsaw, Lodz, and Krakow. The one in Krakow (near the river, close to where Schindler's factory stood and where the wartime ghetto had been locked around the Jews of that ancient city) was isolated and gated, inaccessible that day. We walked around its wrought iron fence and glimpsed the names and dates on the monuments. Most were from the late nineteenth through the early twentieth centuries. This was probably when Jews in greater numbers began to move from the smaller towns toward the metropolis, the long ago capital of royal Poland, still rich in historic buildings, castles, and statues.

The one cemetery (rarely seen by tourists) I visited in Warsaw was a wreck. Every single one of the thousands of headstones (mostly twentieth century) had been leveled and now leaned on each other like fallen dominoes. A truck must have come one night and run them all down, trying to kill their memory by severing even the dead's connection with the land. Henrik, who became my guide in Warsaw, chose to bring me to this cemetery. Born a Jew, he had been hidden as a boy by good Polish Catholics and adopted as one of their own; he looked and sounded (in English) like Mr. Nitsky. He sorrowed at the destruction to the Jewish past contained in the disorder of the cemetery. As we wandered among the acres of destruction we read the *mourner's kaddish* (the Hebrew prayer for the dead, which I had remembered to bring with me from the United States) which he did not really know, and I wondered at the source of this need to destroy even a dead past. Here surely was the sharpest anti-Semitism that I encountered, hatred without a face.

In the Lodz cemetery, which I visited on the final day of my extraordinary stay in my parents' city, the rich manufacturers had constructed large memorials to themselves in death just as they had built grand palaces in life. One had to look hard to locate the Jewish spirit behind the Greco-Roman temples and Egyptian pyramids to self and to money. These monuments had stood the test of time. Bibi and I wandered this cemetery searching among the many headstones for the names of the two grandfathers who had died a "natural death" from starvation and its associated diseases in the Lodz ghetto in 1941 and 1943. We searched among the small headstones of ordinary people. Here many of the names had been effaced from the stones by rain and wind, and many were covered in harsh nettles that stung our hands and fingers as we tried to remove them from the faces of the stones to search for familiar names. Our Hebrew was just good enough to make out names where these were still visible. We never found my grandfathers. We did, however, find two recent monuments, grand in their own way with brass plaques, that almost certainly belonged to my mother's cousin Basia Debski and her husband, Isaak, the only relatives who stayed in Poland after the war; they had clung to their ancestral homes, despite communist pogroms and the drive toward Israel that pushed most remaining Jews out of Poland in the past fifty years. I, who could not remember her name before I left for Poland, knew when I found her burial place as the name came hurtling toward me from the past and from her tomb. I left a rock (in the Jewish style) on the lower edge in memory of a woman I had known only as the recipient of packages my mother sent in the 1950s and from the picture she sent of herself and her husband at my grandfather's grave. My mother's cousin, Basia, visited the grave over which my uncle Jerry had erected a monument when he returned to Poland immediately at the end of the war, with an adjacent stone set at a ninety degree angle, to commemorate my grandmother's death, though not her burial place. When I saw the picture as a child, I told my mother that it clearly showed two graves, but my mother corrected me and noted that the one for her mother was, in her words, "an empty tomb." We discovered several such empty tombs in the Lodz cemetery though none belonged to my grandparents. Basia and my mother had been frequent correspondents, as my mother labored away in the evenings on those thin blue aerograms (covering every inch) trying to keep up connections to any kin who might still be alive. My presence at Basia's grave brought back those childhood memories of this correspondence. As a child, my connection to a past I had not known was often through these feather-light letters that came and went in several languages. Every time I saw one, I realized that the past was still part of our lives. Thus, I knew that Basia had two children, an older daughter and a younger son. Eventually, the son went to Israel, while the daughter, having married a Polish film director, stayed in Lodz. She, no doubt, had dedicated these two large flat grave markers.

Bibi and I spent hours wandering among the tombs, grand and small of Lodz's past, the burial places of people from my family, and it felt right and peaceful to be among them.[1] We had not succeeded in finding either of my grandfathers, whom we had come to locate, but we felt like this place was fully ours.

Other burial places did not feel peaceful, though their present sites might be just as still. At Chelmno, several hours ride from Lodz by taxicab, I found a past my parents had not mentioned, even in hushed tones, a past kept secret. Here was a killing ground to which thousands of Jews from Lodz and innumerable smaller places in the vicinity were sent to be expunged. At Chelmno I found not individual names but whole

1.   I did not know then as I do now that a woman who was likely my mother's grand-mother, Blima Nawry, was buried in Lodz in 1898, probably in this same cemetery.

towns, cities, and peoples (the Jews of Luxembourg, for example) who had been gassed in large vans with the truck's own exhaust fumes. All these people were then dumped into vast pits in the ground, the ground where we now stood. As the earth swelled with the rank putrefaction of so many bodies buried at once, the Germans sought more efficient and hygienic means of disposal. In response, the Nazis had erected early crematoria as they sought new ways to dispose of corpses, methods carefully studied by those officials who would eventually mechanize, systematize, and perfect the process of death in Auschwitz and other places. More than two hundred thousand Jews, including, most likely, my mother's three-year-old son, taken away in the roundup of young children and old people in 1942, had been put to death in this terrible place. Here, too, I found the names of places like Piebenice, Lask, and above all Zdunska Wola, a name I had not heard since my mother spoke it with her American aunt years and years ago. It was the small city from which I thought I remembered that my mother's older brother's wife had come. It was Chelmno, I realized that day, to which most of that family had come to die. I now know that Zdunska Wola, known for the lilacs my mother loved, was a city of innumerable Sieradzkis,[2] some probably my mother's cousins, aunts, and uncles. Chelmno may also have been the place to which various members of my mother's mother's family (the Nawrys) had come—or was it to Treblinka because my grandmother's family came from a city closer to Warsaw? Prolific, like the Sieradzkis, that family had once bred eleven sisters and a brother (a rich stocking manufacturer) and all their children and children's children. There had been plenty of them to go to various places, Chelmno among them. Here, most likely, those three little cousins of my mother's in their pretty cotton summer dresses, which I remembered from a tiny picture we once had, were taken to be smothered alongside their parents, helping the earth to swell. And it might have been this place to which my mother's

2. I saw these long lists of Sieradzkis, variously spelled, on an internet site for Polish Jewish genealogy, discovered several years after my visit.

uncle, the rabbi and town leader, had been sent. When ordered by the Nazis who stormed the town to produce a list for selection, he told them that he needed until morning to comply. He came alone early the next morning in his prayer shawl (*talit*) with a Torah in his arms to die alone. He had not saved anyone, but he had not lost his soul either. (The story had been retold in the *Jewish Daily Forward* just after we arrived in New York City.) The story is one I had remembered clearly as a child, a child who needed some sense of righteousness.

The area around Lodz had been alive with towns like the one from which he came and those listed on the wall at Chelmno, many towns with odd-sounding names. In the early nineteenth century, when Sieradzkis were already long settled in the region, the city of Lodz was hardly more than a stop on the road to the city of Pyotrkow. The important smaller cities in this region, called the Wielkopolska (large or grand Poland) existed in a line that connected Kalisz in the West, through towns like Zdunska Wola toward Piotrkow and beyond that toward Radom in the east. My mother often mentioned these and other tributary centers off this line, such as Tomaszow and Pabianice, all of them vibrant centers of Jewish life in Poland. In the late nineteenth century the smaller cities of this region were eventually absorbed into the great city's orbit as Lodz became Poland's booming center of manufacturing, a major metropolis of more than one-half million people (second in size only to Warsaw), and a center of Jewish urban life. According to the *Encyclopedia of Jewish Life Before and During the Holocaust*, Jews settled in the Lodz district at the end of the eighteenth century and within a short period of time "dominated economic life, mainly in trade and crafts." The first synagogue was built in 1809. It seems that Sieradzkis were there from this very earliest period. Not long after that first synagogue was built, *Bluma Sieradzki*, a woman with my mother's name, and perhaps a distant relative, was born in 1830.

Another town, and one whose marker we passed in the taxicab on the way to Chelmno, was Sieradz, from which my grandfather's family had almost certainly borrowed its name, though he himself was born in Lask (in the same Lodz district). My connection to this place had thus been passed on to my mother and my uncle, down to the many school documents which asked for mother's maiden name. These town names are still marked in the region around Lodz. But the Jews are gone, except those hundreds of thousands who still fester in the ground beneath Chelmno, unremembered by name and usually unvisited even by tourists.

Auschwitz is different. A museum of death on the standard tourist route, visited by organized tours and tour groups from everywhere. After our first day in Krakow, Bibi and I took the train to Auschwitz, which is not far away. We shared a cab from the train with a young Japanese man and an American medical resident (with a German name); and we met a Canadian couple at the train platform when we returned to Krakow. People from everywhere come to Auschwitz. It was a place that I dreaded to visit because of its personal and historical associations. History has turned Auschwitz into a symbol that transcends the millions of individuals gassed, beaten, and worked to death in its real space. Bibi was struck by the fact that the famous gate with its well-known lie "Arbeit Macht Frei," is smaller than one imagined it to be. And she is right; it is pictured so often in books and on film that it has become huge in our minds. The Auschwitz we visit today is a much mediated experience, a carefully administered memory center. The day we went was unexpectedly cold and drizzly, and we were underdressed. The physical discomfort seemed appropriate to the occasion and to our thoughts, and the cold made us miserable and cranky with each other. We held each other, Bibi and I, for warmth and comfort. I wore my hat the entire time, remembering to cover my head in this place, made sacred by death and personal memory but otherwise revolting.

It is difficult to maintain one's own thoughts when confronted by Auschwitz as a museum. The name alone conjures up supreme evil, and the museum's displays of hair, shoes, bowls, and photographs, are a horror-house version of charnel reality. But Birkenau, the newer paired

campsite set up exclusively for Jewish extermination, in its vast auster-
ity with its flat toiletless wooden barracks and unspoken gate, made me
remember the stories my mother told. The stories were often of keeping
part of your bread ration as a pillow and sleeping with your soup bowl
held tight so that these would not be stolen at night. The larger the bowl
the more soup it could hold and you might urge the person who ladled
it to add something to the usual portion. The exhibit at Auschwitz that
spoke to me most deeply was the vast collection of metal bowls—of every
size and color—the expression of basic need and of a connection with
life's nurture. There was, my father told me, a great competition over the
larger of these bowls, remaindered (as were shoes) after their possessors'
deaths. The inmates, dreaming of tomorrow's soupy water, clutched in
sleep these bowls, passed along over the life of the camp, and still there
as material witness.

We saw, too, the little front room for the overseeing guard, with its
own private stove, and on this very chilly day, even in May, I remembered
the bitter cold in midwinter Poland after my parents passed through the
entrance to Birkenau, and my father's stories of night time *Appells*, when
all the inmates were gathered, counted, and culled.

―――――

Throughout our visit to Poland, I was eager to eat food I thought would
stimulate my memory, and I was betrayed by the reality. My mother was
an excellent cook in the traditional Jewish style, and I thought (wrongly)
that this was probably an adaptation of the local Polish cuisine. At a
"good" restaurant in Warsaw's old town we ordered borscht; I expected the
ruby red liquid I had always loved and which Bibi too had come to enjoy.
Instead, we received a dun colored, cabbage thickened stew with sausages.
Throughout the twelve days of our visit to Poland, food, the very quick of
memory, turned out not to be what I expected. Polish food, leaden with
pork, tasted nothing like the kosher food I knew, except for the wonderful
bread and herring, *chleb* and *sledz*, two words I remembered even before

I left for Poland. These uncooked staples were common to Poles and Jews and remain a link today. Bibi and I had to seek out a Jewish style restaurant in Krakow to get a slight taste of home and memory. Clearly, in the matter of cuisine, the division between Jews and non Jews in prewar Poland had been sharp. Jews who kept kosher (almost certainly the great majority) ate at home or among their own people and kept their tastes separate as in the rabbinic injunctions. They had probably few occasions to absorb Polish cooking, and Polish indulgences, including alcoholic ones, remained a world apart. Maybe only in the cafes and in the pastry shops could Jews grab a small piece of the local action. Indeed, Polish cakes, such as apple cake (so unlike American apple pie) did bring back sweet memories of one of my mother's specialties.

No, food was not a chord my memory could play, but smell was, especially the smell of certain trees, like the intoxicating acacia. These were blooming luxuriously in Chelmno, where their taunting fragrance mixed with that of the wild roses. My mother always talked about the acacia and brought any similar fragrance to my attention whenever she detected it in the United States. Even more than the acacia, my mother adored the smell of lilacs, which usually pervades the Polish spring air with its April profusion, but we had come too late in the year for that. We did find the grand flowering chestnut trees and walked in their deep shade. These trees and plants and the visual sensations of the great parks in Warsaw and Lodz and treed boulevards in Krakow had to compensate for food that was always mediocre and never like home.

And there was language. I went to Poland without a tongue and returned with Polish ringing in my ears. As a child, I had learned Polish, as I had learned German and Yiddish, by listening. But unlike these, I had never learned to speak Polish. I knew Polish only as an interloper, by listening in on adult conversations, usually between my mother and my uncle or my uncle and aunt. My parents never spoke to me or to each other in Polish, and I was never called on to use it so for me it never became a real spoken language. This language without a tongue came back to me in Poland, after just a few days of immersion in its sounds. When I first arrived, I could understand only a word here and there. Then, it came back to me all at once, as a whole language, something I first noticed in that Warsaw department store. Polish had always been a foreign language to me, and in Poland it remained a foreign language, but it was a familiar foreign language. I heard it everywhere, and throughout my visit to Poland I felt as if I was continuously eavesdropping on conversations. I wanted to tell people just to speak to me because I could understand them, even if I could not communicate with them except in English. I never learned more than to say thank you and good bye and the names of some few things. I also realized that this must have been my father's experience as someone for whom Polish always remained a familiar foreign language.

———

That strange, uneven involvement in the language helped to open my memories, which had disappeared or been hidden, like the language, behind a screen. During the entire time I was in Poland, I was inundated with specific remembrances of incidents, people, names, which I had not thought about for decades; I also remembered things told to me by my parents or their friends. I had vivid recollections of childhood scenes—sharp memories of my parents—and I heard long-forgotten voices. These fragments of the unremembered past were now suddenly available to the present. They pleasantly haunted me. The whole time I was in Poland, I lived a double life: a tourist in the present and a visitor to the past. I dozed in the afternoons, exhausted by the rigors of living in both past and present that came with this resumption of language. Then I would dream of these same people and things, thus being three times immersed. Even sleep was not sleep, only a place for more memories. I often shared these experiences with Bibi for whom the people I remembered remained entirely foreign, not even ghosts.

And there were places—visual sensations of things I had never seen, but had been often told about. I was especially nervous about going to Lodz; through the endless stories Lodz was as familiar to me as a child as was the Brooklyn I actually inhabited. My mother had loved the city of her youth and described it in vivid detail. Lodz was for her alive with desire. She had told me about the life of the deep courtyards, full of children and courting couples. She had described street arrangements, shops and restaurants, cinemas, and streetcars. Now in the real city, my heart throbbed when I encountered the busy avenue where many street car lines converged and people gathered to catch the *tramwaj* (tram). I walked past and into courtyards where one could sit and drink tea.

I had decided to stay at the Hotel Grand on *ul* Piotrkowska, aspiring to a place that had excluded Jews before the war and at which my mother could hardly have dreamed of registering. The place was famous for its movie-star visitors (the prewar Poles, including my mother, loved the movies), and even while we were there, Roman Polanski, the Polish-American director, was registered as a guest. The dining room included large photos drawn from cinema history. But arriving by taxi cab from the station onto *ul* Piotrkowska where the hotel sits, close to my mother's childhood home, was both a shock and a delight. This heart of Lodz was far smaller and Piotrkowska less grand than I had expected. Very little had changed physically. Lodz had been spared bombardment during the war, and I had come before its probable European Union modernization. It seemed at once utterly familiar and completely strange. The street was very wide and the buildings, though grown shabby, very elaborate in their late nineteenth-century grandeur, though less tall than I had imagined. Some of the huge apartment buildings were in the streets just behind the Piotrkowska. My father had spoken of these *kamienicas* (large stone apartment buildings) with awe, and I always assumed that he was exaggerating; I discovered, however, that he had in fact told the truth, and they were massive and ornate. It was amazing to be in the city in which my mother had been born and lived, to see the balconies and the courtyards as she had known them, to sit in the cafes and *cukiernias* (sweet shops) of her youth. Finally, in Lodz, I began to feel strangely at home as my childhood imaginings began to flourish among the dilapidated stones of my parent's lives.

Lodz had always been broken in my mind into two parts, my mother's Lodz and my father's Lodz. And so it was when I visited it in May 2000. Beyond what is today the *plac Wolnosci* (Liberation plaza) which concludes Lodz's Champs Elysées of the Piotrkowska, beyond Poznanski's vast brick manufacturing complex (which I unfortunately did not visit) where the textile workers were housed behind his own grand private palace, lay the old Jewish ghetto of Lodz, and beyond this on its furthest fringe, the Balut of my father's childhood memories. This was once an infamous and only semi-incorporated part of the great city. And my mother used to shudder when my father fondly recalled the life of those who inhabited this district. During the German occupation and incorporation of Lodz, the Jewish ghetto and Balut more particularly became the intended habitation of *all* the Jews of the city and many more besides when the Nazis converted Lodz into their own manufactury of war materièl and death. Before the war, Balut had been ramshackle and mostly poor. In appearance today it seemed much the same. As Bibi and I departed from elegant, if also rundown and over-the-hill manufacturing Lodz (my mother's city) past the park and entered my father's part of the city, my memory was ignited—ignited by the sight and the smell of poverty, once Jewish and now otherwise (but also often foreign). The heart of the district is the *Nowe Ryneck* (once Balut market)—a huge, open-air market, where everything can be bought and sold: fruits, vegetables, and meats, clothes (new and used), old clock radios, iron nails, cosmetics, and used plumbing fittings. It is a lively, even bustling, place spilling over at the edges with vitality, but it is locked up in the most rundown, ill-used housing stock—some of it recently built (by the Communists after the war), but much still a reminder of my father's past. Toward this rundown district, old and dilapidated even in 1940, the Nazis slammed Jewish humanity and locked it first behind guarded gates, then behind overpasses, locking them out eventually even from the more salubrious parts of the old ghetto and swelling the remaining district's population from 30,000 to more than 150,000 people, whom they then systematically starved. My father had lived and started to prosper here (how was it possible?) before the war. He had been born here, gone to *heder* here, and started to work here (no doubt among such stalls) by eight years of age. He had also raised a family of four children close by, who had "almost survived the war," because he had hidden them amidst the ghetto's maze of streets and alleys and behind the protection that payoffs to the right people could bring. Here, too, he had hidden his diamonds, of which I thought very briefly as I walked the streets and wondered where exactly they might be. Were they still somewhere underneath an outhouse or some communist-era structure as he had presumed? Had they been found by a lucky stranger, digging in the ghetto muck?

It made me shudder to walk through this part of Lodz. Something about Balut and my father's life here made this place very different than my mother's part, much harder to play just the tourist, even the historical tourist. It was more than the fact of the deadly ghetto it had become under German occupation. I thought of it as a burial ground. He had buried his diamonds here and hidden his children, and he recovered neither from the past. I understood why he had laughed at my childish suggestions about digging for his buried treasure. I shuddered at the sacredness of the place and the pain that remembering the past brought him. Though we were very thirsty and we were tempted, Bibi and I could buy nothing here, not even a drink on a hot, hot day. Not until we had passed out of the thick of the place where my father and mother had spent four years of the war and where so much suffering had taken place, did we dare to buy a couple of cokes on the open vista of the much smaller "old market" square as we looked across the park, toward respectable Lodz.

Lodz, like every other part of Poland that I saw, is rich in churches (including the old reformed Protestant Church at the corner of the plac Wolnosci that had only the year we were there, in 2000, been converted to Catholicism). These churches I could not enter. Bibi and I went into churches even in Krakow, out of historical and aesthetic interest (as we did in Italy or France), but not in Lodz. The old anti-Semitic memories could not be so easily quelled by current calm. (At Easter time, my mother always said, it was dangerous for a Jew even to be seen on the streets near a church, and Jews would hide during this season to avoid any possible provocation.) The churches that loomed up in Lodz were actually readily eclipsed in our sight lines by the many ornamental cupolas that the Lodz manufacturers had attached to their secular apartment houses and palaces—the Jewish and German answer to the Polish Catholic church—intended to be just as eye-catching and splendid.

In Lodz I felt most connected to the past. There amidst its rich contradictions, my mind resettled into the past, there between my father's Lodz and my mother's.

———

Before leaving the United States, I had carefully arranged to give a talk at the American Studies Institute at the University of Lodz. I was at once eager to maintain some connection with the person I have become—a professor and an Americanist—and to make contact with my present-day colleagues. This turned out to be a shrewd move not only because my academic hosts, Elzbieta Oleksy and her husband Wiesiek, were wonderful people who displayed Polish courtesy at its finest and most sincere but also because the students I met helped me to negotiate the archives of birth in Lodz.

I arrived laden with my books, four of them, hoping to leave in Lodz a piece of myself as I have become, while taking back pieces of the people from whom I came. This perfect exchange was very American in its gesture of pride in self-creation. Depositing my books at the university, the very pinnacle of Polish learning (though Lodz's university was created after the war in 1945), was meant especially as a tribute to my father who could read and write the Latin script on which Polish (and English) is based only with difficulty. I loved the thought of them on some library bookshelf, in all their wordiness, a monument to the names lost in the murky soils of Chelmo and Auschwitz, names that possessed neither Latin nor Hebrew inscriptions for remembrance, names that lacked tombs and markings of any kind.

The students I met there, especially Marek and Janna, spoke English beautifully and were beautiful physically as well. And they were respectful of my desires. Marek and Janna served as spokespersons at the municipal archives of births and deaths the morning after my visit to the university, where I had spoken about the lost Lindbergh child. (This building was later reclaimed because it had been a Jewish residence before the war.) I also brought Bibi, who had not come to my lecture the previous day, with me to the archives.

I was looking for birth certificates for my father, my mother, and their children. By some stroke of foresight, I had written down the children's names one evening when my mother and I were sitting around the kitchen table in Brooklyn and I asked her for them. These names had *never* been spoken in our house. My mother spoke them this one and only time because I explained to her that "I want them for the future." I had put the list of names in my passport case and had not looked at them since. I took the list out just before I left for Poland: Wolf, Brandel, Schepsel, Abraham, Henja. By the time I got to Lodz, I needed no cue cards but could remember all the names as if they had been my childhood familiars. I wrote their names, my parents' names and approximate dates of birth for each child (all of them completely made up, except for my mother's son who, I knew, had been born in June 1939). It turned out that I had misspelled my mother's previous married name, spelling it as she had, Krimalowska (in Polish records the first three vowels had all become o's) but the archivist, whose resourcefulness was as admirable as her good will and eagerness to help me, found the certificate anyway. She needed twenty-four hours to dig into what she called the "old Jewish records." (These Jewish records, like Jews themselves, were kept separately in Poland.)

The next day, when I returned, I paid twenty-five zloty for each of the precious pieces of paper she handed me. As a by-product, I learned the names of my father's first wife and my mother's first husband for the first time. In my excitement and because I was with Janna and Marek, I did not want to take too much time lingering over the documents. I did notice hastily that the dates of birth for my parents were somewhat odd, but ignored this for the time being and concentrated instead on the certificates that confirmed the births of my siblings— three brothers and two sisters. I both laughed and cried at once, a mixture of emotions completely true to my mood. I had found them, confirmed their existence, only to be stunned now by the much more real fact of their destruction. My sisters and brothers, those phantoms of my own childhood, had been born and lived in Lodz, where I was now, but they were not.

Only later, after we left Lodz to go south to Krakow and to Auschwitz, following the route of at least two of them (only this time in first-class rail carriages like proper tourists) did I realize that I had not looked for the birth certificates of either my wonderful uncle Jerry, who helped to shape my life, or my uncle Avrum, whom I never knew but for whom my mother mourned all her life. I had also not looked for the birth certificate of Avrum's daughter (was it Wanda, maybe?) whom I only knew as *das einikl* (the grandchild) beloved by the whole household that lived together, always close before the war, and then in those last years jammed together in the increasingly decrepit, starving, and tomblike ghetto of Lodz. Today, as a historical tourist, I could just leave it all behind, the city and the ghetto created to encircle and enslave the Jewish community of the entire Lodz district. But sixty years ago, leaving was much harder than arriving, and Jews left only in wheelbarrows or cattle cars. *Das einikle*, who I now know to have been called *Chana Sieradzka*, left together with my mother, my grandmother Pola, and my uncle Avrum to Auschwitz. They were all very eager to make Chana look older (she was not yet 13).[3] Only my mother survived.

3. By putting together several records, I concluded that my cousin was named Chana Sieradzka and born on October 3, 1931. She lived until the deportation to Auschwitz in August 1944, with her family on Hohenstrasse 36 in the Lodz Ghetto.

CHAPTER 2

I NEVER HAD
GRANDPARENTS

The old and the young were least likely to survive the ghetto, its many selections, or the final command to the left at the entrance to Auschwitz-Birkenau. Both my parents had photographs of their parents, carefully framed and always on display in their bedroom. They are a vivid and indelible part of my childhood. I used to stare at these photos for hours to give them a kind of imagined life. In this sense I was a historian before I could read by using whatever still remained to reconstruct the past. I always knew that I did not have living grandparents. They had disappeared in the great conflagration. As a child in Germany most other children also did not have grandparents so only after I came to the United States did I begin to feel the deprivation. Most of my schoolmates had at least one grandparent, and we were often asked to list the names of grandparents on required school forms. As a result, it became necessary for me to begin to explain.

The one and only clear memory I have about first grade at P.S. 54 in Brooklyn was going from teacher to teacher to tell them "the story." I was five years old, a very young storyteller, but I told them what I knew and the teachers seemed eager to listen. My own teacher sent me to another, who then sent me to another, until the story was told all around the school. I even told the story to a group in the teachers' special space. The devil, I told them, had taken my grandparents, and many others, and all of them were consumed in flames. The devil's name was Hitler, and he had chosen the Jews, for no reason except that they were Jews. It was, a miracle, I assured them, that my parents had survived. My life, too, was a kind of miracle, a child born out of the ashes of destruction.

I often considered the peculiar *glick-imglick* (luck-misfortune) of my birth: I was the product of an unparalleled disaster that it was my fate to reflect upon for the rest of my life. I would never have been born, if the Hitler-devil had not redirected the course of history. That terrible history was the basis for my creation, and there was no getting around the fact that my origins lay in catastrophe. Yet I was also a kind of salvation to my parents, a means to move from the unredeemable past into a possible future. At one time my parents had their parents and their own children simultaneously, the way it was meant to be, *dor va dor* (from generation to generation) as it says in the Hebrew *sidur* (prayer book).

Left: My grandmother, Pola Nawry Sieradzki, in Poland around the turn of the twentieth century, said to be taken around the time of her marriage. Right: My grandfather, Israel Sieradzki, in Poland around the turn of the twentieth century.

Now my parents had come together to create a new family around me. But there were no grandparents.

The photographs allowed me to imagine grandparents, but not to play or talk with them or learn from them as other children did. Because my mother was a good storyteller, most of my imagining centered on her parents, *Perla (Pola) Nawry Sieradzki* and *Israel Fawel Sieradzki*. Their photos were of young people. Taken either just before or just after their marriage, these pictorial documents created a truncated past. I always pictured them that way—young, very dark haired, with blazing black eyes, and full of a future. Many years later I came across a photo of my much older grandmother, but I could not recognize her and sought (as I still seek) to put the two pictures together, to see how the younger woman became the haggard, white-haired woman pictured in the Lodz ghetto.

My mother had not known her own grandmother and, when I was a child, this was somehow eerily comforting. It is not comforting now to think of this as a family tradition. Like most Eastern European Jews, who were named after important dead relations, my mother was named after her grandmother Blima[1] (the Yiddish form), as my daughter is named after her grandmother (my mother) Bluma, whom she never knew. I am named after my grandmother, Pola, whom I did not know. Is it my future granddaughter's fate to be named Paula also, after me, and likewise not to know her grandmother?

My grandmother Pola was born in 1879, as my mother told me long ago, a date remembered all those years probably because I was so strongly drawn to this woman whose name I bore. When I was in Lodz, I located a ghetto document and learned that her birthday was June 24. It is not

---

1.   I found that a Blima Newry was buried in Lodz Province (Piotrkow Gubernia) in 1898. This is likely my mother's grandmother, my great grandmother, since the date of death would coincide well with the age at which my mother's grandmother would have died after giving birth to her twelve children, the first of whom (my grandmother) was born in 1879.

at all certain that this is a precise birth-date because East European Jews usually remembered their birthdays according to the Jewish calendar and then loosely translated this date into the Christian form. Many documents lie this way, and all documents are only proximate reflections of experience just as photos provide only a glancing resemblance. The historian can find little real certainty in these human facsimiles. On that same document, her *Anmeldung* (registration) in the Litzmannstadt (Lodz) Ghetto—the Nazis changed the name of the city (and the names of its streets) when they integrated it into the Reich—I saw her signature for the first time. This was a far more personal expression of the grandmother I never knew and provided me with a new representation to go along with the photograph. It was a beautiful signature—clear, strong, and steady, with lovely embellishments on the "S" and the "z."

In her photograph, my grandmother wears a high Victorian hairdo (possibly a wig, if the picture was taken after she was married because orthodox Jewish women are required to cover their heads after marriage) and a very high-necked dark dress with a small round pin at the center. She looks elegant, very pretty, and intense. The photograph has been romanticized, both by the photographer and by me, but the intensity was her own. My grandmother's nickname (in her family of twelve children) was the "empress," not the princess or the queen, but grander still. The oldest of the children, she was seen in larger than life terms. She spoke several languages. Among these was Polish, which, according to my mother, she learned secretly, in the basement of her house, where students and teacher hid to evade Russian officials who were trying to stamp out Polish nationalism. Clearly my grandmother, in her secular knowledge and eagerness to learn Polish, identified with those Jews who saw possibilities for themselves in a reborn Poland.

As the oldest daughter, she had helped to raise a large family long before she was married and even before her own mother died (in childbirth or soon after the youngest was born). She had clear capabilities and large expectations about life. And she married for love, a very rare occurrence in an Orthodox Jewish culture where respectable girls were matched up and personal inclination was at most a marginal consideration. She had seen my grandfather—young, dark, handsome, with soulful eyes (or so he seems in his photo)—on a balcony across the courtyard in the large apartment house where they both lived. And they had fixated on each other. He was softer, kinder, and gentler in character with a Hasidic metaphysical inclination. Intoxicated with God, he also become intoxicated with her. Of the two parents, my mother loved her father best, and her preference made her mother all the more fascinating to me.

My grandmother was not an easy woman to please, and it was easier, in traditional Jewish families, for sons to please their mothers anyway. My mother apparently never fully succeeded with her own mother. (This may be why my mother always gave me the sense of strong approval that has sustained me.) Pola wanted her daughter to be well educated, well dressed, well wed. My mother resisted. She, who cared more about spiritual beauty than surface beauty, only did the last well enough for her mother, and even this fairly late. My mother was pretty enough as a girl, as was clear in another photo salvaged from the wreckage of postwar Poland, but she was neither striking nor beautiful (see photograph on p. 127). My mother also had her fill of other things to do, things her own mother did not want to do, such as cooking, baking, and organizing the household. My grandmother largely turned the cooking over to my mother when she was just eleven or twelve. Pola always said (and my mother repeated to me) that a woman needed to know how to run a household well, no matter how many servants she might someday have. My mother's family never had servants (*mishorsim*), an absence that marked their status. People of means had servants; other people had daughters. My grandmother may have given my mother many responsibilities as a form of training in wifely duties or because she herself had done so much of it as the oldest daughter that she had tired of the duties. My mother did them very well, loving her father and her two brothers as she did.

Given her housekeeping experience and her extraordinary memory, in the 1960s my mother could still remember the price of flour and sugar in Lodz in the 1920s. She described to me how she made purchases at the local markets and the small quantities (in grams) she bought of precious commodities like butter; she could run a household well and economically. And she could set a table fit for a queen. (I used to tell her that "Queen Elizabeth could come to your dinner parties.") My mother learned to do all these things very well in part because her own mother had very high standards and expectations.

It was no easy task to run an orthodox, kosher household in Poland between the wars when chickens were still selected live by the buyer, then slaughtered and plucked; the dough for bread and *challahs* (Sabbath bread) was made at home and brought on certain days to bake in the baker's ovens; everything had to shine before the Sabbath candles were lit, and the shine was even more glowing on the holidays. In these households no fire was ever lit on *Shabbos* or the holidays, but food needed to be served anyway. And it was not easy when the men ate first and separately in the *Succah* (the outdoor hut constructed during the Feast of Tabernacles) of the best there was, and the women only ate much later from the leftovers. It is difficult to imagine my empress grandmother, with her secular languages and access to more enlightened beliefs, satisfied by such treatment, but it is equally hard to see how she could have avoided it once she had chosen to marry a Hasid.

Like many orthodox Jewish women, my grandmother had worked when she first married and before the children were born, while my grandfather spent a few years in advanced learning in traditional Jewish texts. She had followed in her family's business of selling luxury goods while my grandfather gathered together with other disciples of the *Gere Rebbe* (Rabbi of Ger). The *Gere* was one of the many great Hasidic seers who dominated religious life through most of Eastern Europe in the nineteenth century, and he was one of the most widely followed in central Poland in the early twentieth century. With its ecstatic qualities and intense pietism, Hasidism also emphasized the magical qualities of the *Rebbe* and created inherited dynastic traditions around these "saints" (*Zaddikim*). Many Hasidim deemphasized traditional learning and gave priority to spiritual and mystical attainments. The Polish sect that gathered around the Rabbi of Ger, centered in the Warsaw area, was much more restrained and intellectual than the tradition that developed in the Ukraine and other parts of the Russian Pale. The followers of the Rabbi of Ger integrated the learned rabbinical traditions with Hasidic spiritual orientation and placed far less emphasis on the personal healing powers of the rebbe. When he was young, my grandfather met with other young men in the *shtieblech* (small study rooms) that dotted the Jewish landscapes of the city and *stetl* culture. They read, studied, meditated, and argued with each other on points that were mediated by older scholars and occasionally settled by either the seer himself or more likely one of his immediate circle. Thus was Jewish learning passed on, from generation to generation. By the time he had his picture taken, my grandfather Israel already had a neatly trimmed beard and wore a Jewish hat (*Yiddish hitl*), not the long beard and *stramel* (wide velvet or fur trimmed black hat) of Jewish orthodox tradition. This might have been a result of my grandmother's influence or simply a function of the changes taking place even among Hasidim during this time.

My grandfather, who was born in 1880, thus already reflected some of the complex reality among Polish orthodox Jews by the early twentieth century. He was a faithful and somewhat otherworldly Jew, but he nevertheless married a woman who was educated in secular subjects and, from my mother's descriptions of him, was the soul of kindness and reason. He did not shun her or other women as orthodox men were enjoined to do. She often got his attention and affection. His own children moved out of the Hasidic orbits within which he had traveled. He wore modern conservative dress, not the long satin coats (*zadine yibitze*) of the Hasidim. He was, my mother told me, "modern Orthodox" in the terms of his time. But probably his own father and grandfather had dressed in that more traditional garb, and my mother could still name each of the individual clothing items, probably because she had seen and learned about them from relatives who still were fully immersed in that other world, people she met at weddings and other important occasions.

When her children started to arrive, my grandmother retreated into her household, although my sense is that she never entirely gave up trading to some extent. She did not have a wealthy father to support my grandfather's further studies, as would have been the case among those whose families had money and servants. Smart and pretty, she no doubt was very good at her commercial activities. Before my mother's oldest brother *Abram (Avrum) Sieradzki* was born, she bore two children, only to lose them soon after childbirth. Then the three siblings I know about came in quick succession, two or three years apart: my uncle Avrum on October 9, 1908 (according to his *Anmeldung* in the Lodz ghetto), my mother, Bluma Reisl, on February 1, 1910 (according to her birth certificate), and then my uncle Jerry (Jehuda) on March 10, 1913 (according to his death certificate). Just after uncle Jerry's birth my grandfather came to America to seek a better life for himself and his family than was possible in stagnant Poland where Jewish men were being reduced to begging or to work as day laborers as part of the general impoverishment of the Jewish masses in Poland before the first world war. Israel came to work alongside my grandmother's sister's (Toby Weill) husband in the lower East Side of New York. When I asked her what kind of work my grandfather did in New York, my mother said that "he probably worked at a pushcart," hoping to move up from there as so many others did. But while most Jews who came to the United States stayed and eventually prospered (*dor va dor*), my grandfather returned to Poland.

He returned to Poland because my grandmother summoned him back. According to my mother, she would not cross the ocean with the young children unescorted. Israel had to come for her so he returned to Poland, never again to reach the United States. The war shattered normal life in Europe and disrupted migration to America. After the war the new immigration restriction legislation, which passed first in 1921 and then more permanently in 1924, shut off almost all immigration from Eastern Europe. History, I tell my students, is about all of us and it affects each of us. Even I, a stranger to this country, had a part to play. History is also unpredictable. My grandfather came to New York like so many others. Had it not been for my grandmother's insistence that he return, my mother might have grown up in the United States to become a part of my study of second-generation immigrants in American schools in the 1920s. Instead, my grandfather and his family were caught in Europe permanently, and as a result I was born in Europe. After another forty years, I came in my grandfather's wake, but only after history had taken its heavy toll.

My grandfather did not abandon my grandmother as did some men who planted their feet firmly in the *goldene medina* (golden land) and started a new American family. Nor did Israel's family follow him as did the great majority of other Jewish families. He was a man of integrity, and he loved Pola. But that decision sealed their fate.

Life in Poland had been difficult even before World War I, but the war brought real suffering. Both of my parents were old enough to remember the poverty they endured during these very hard times. Poland, and within it Lodz, were battle sites during that war, and in Poland the war lasted beyond the 1918 truce that officially ended the engagements in the western theater, the only ending we usually learn about in American schools. In central Europe, the newly created Soviet Union sent troops to claim as much of Poland as possible before the Treaty of Versailles would make Poland into an independent nation once again, as the empires of Germany, Austria-Hungary and Russia were dissolved into history, spilling their ethnicities onto a new map of Europe. This situation probably encouraged my grandmother's renewed trading activities.

My grandmother's sights were set on a better life. And she frequently imagined that her honor was bruised or slighted. Apparently, once when she attended a family wedding, she refused to eat because her plate (alone of all the plates!) was chipped. She was a woman whose sense of dignity was strong, but this temperament inevitably led to much disappointment. My mother, the middle child and the only daughter, did not become like her mother. In her native modesty, she followed in her admired father's spiritual path and chose to see how much she had rather than what others did and she lacked. ("Every misfortune has some buried fortune," she frequently reminded me. Because my whole life could be viewed this way, I understood.) But I loved my grandmother, with all her faults, without ever knowing her, and because my mother's humility sometimes annoyed me, I fashioned myself, in part, according to what my mother told me of her own mother and my namesake. I, too, expected much even as a child whose daily family life was a reminder of my good fortune just to be alive. In that terrible ghetto photo of my grandmother, my mother also appears. Unlike my grandmother, who even in adversity stares straight at the photographer, my mother's face is turned to the side, shy of the camera, not about to make a fuss even about this terrible place. My mother had a very different sense of dignity than my grandmother.

The ghetto, which tormented all its inhabitants, must have been especially humiliating to my grandmother who always, even when they had very little, insisted that the family live in the "good" part of Lodz, in an elegant apartment building in neighborhoods that were not exclusively Jewish. With her knowledge of Polish and German, she could live amidst both assimilated Jews and Christians near the *ul* Piotrkowska. From her *Anmeldung* (registration) in the Litzmannstadt ghetto I know that in 1940, when she was forced to live exclusively among Jews in the ghetto, way out on the other side of the city, my grandmother was assigned an apartment containing one room and a kitchen on Hohensteinerstrasse (Zgierska in Polish). Terrible as this was, it was not the worst arrangement because many apartments had no kitchen at all and Hohensteinerstrasse was a main street with some possibility of light from the wide thoroughfare (later she was relocated to Holz Strasse). But it was, of course, very awful. At sixty years of age, twice a grandmother, with her brilliant oldest son and a very respectably married daughter, the situation she faced was undoubtedly a terrible ordeal, even before the starvation, disease, death, and selections began. My mother once told me that in the ghetto my beautiful, dark-haired grandmother turned white overnight. Whatever my grandmother's social aspirations might have been, whatever her family position, whatever her commitments to Polish nationality, she found herself one Jew among the hundreds of thousands of others who were now defined only in this one dimension by authorities for whom being a hated Jew charted a path toward destruction.

They had lived most recently before their forced departure in an apartment on the Radwainska (number 7) with substantial, dark mahogany furniture. My mother recalled a huge armoire and a large dining table and chairs. Avrum and his family lived in the same building. Rapidly, they were all turned out; first, my grandparents moved into the ghetto on February 18, 1940, the same day as my mother, and then my uncle Avrum on March 15th. This was especially galling because he was evicted when his "best friend" (was he a *volksdeutsche*?) brought the German authorities with that special knock on the door and claimed Avrum's apartment and its contents for himself. The ghetto swallowed them all. On June 2, 1940, my grandmother Pola Sieradzka, listed as a "hausfrau," whose religion was "Mose" was registered at the "Litzmannstadt ghetto." Soon after this, the ghetto swelled with Jews, eventually registering 240,000 persons before it was closed officially more than four years later in August 1944. The ghetto did not discriminate between Eastern European Jews and Western European Jews, proud Jews with *yiches* (honor and respect) and Jews from the margins of respectable Jewish society. And one by one, the ghetto authorities selected and streamed them forward into the camps where death was the goal, not just the byproduct of carefully planned humiliation.

I know neither how my grandmother survived through the entire period of the ghetto's operation nor why she was not selected earlier to go to Chelmno or die of disease and starvation. Avrum's knowledge, shrewdness, and possible connections may have helped. "He knew all about calories," my mother told me. I was unclear about the exact details, but Avrum had aspired to becoming a doctor, had some training, and may have been a *felsher* (a special medical position in Eastern Europe where someone trained in medicine without accreditation as a doctor). Because of this study he knew about various nutrients, their work in the process of sustaining life, and blood treatments where a patient's own antibodies were used to counteract disease. Maybe because of this knowledge he was drawn into circles where he gained other kinds of information. Maybe he used his knowledge to spread the rations among them, while his own skills were used in the ghetto hospital. This may have given him access to other kinds of information that spared some members of the family until the end. But the ghetto's blight exceeded his or anyone else's control, and my grandfather Israel starved his way out of Lodz more than a year before the others left for Auschwitz. Even Avrum's knowledge of calories was not enough to save the others from becoming part of the last transport to Auschwitz. In my house while I was growing up, the conversation much more often concerned the ghetto than the camps, probably because both of my parents spent so much more time there and because they had their families around them—the semblance of a real if terrible life, gone once they left.

Of all the means of death, life in the Lodz ghetto is what I knew most about as a child, and the names of the streets that years later I found on maps—Lagiewnicka, Rymarska, Wolborska, Limanowskiego—spun around me. They all had meaning to my parents—places in which they worked or received rations or where they were treated for diseases. These were Polish words even my father knew well. Here were the places to which they went to work or to seek favors or where the names of the next group selected for exit were posted. Here they made decisions about whether to give a cherished pat of butter to a parent or a child, as my mother once explained to me in regard to her father's death. Here they spent the last years of their lives with their fathers and mothers, children, brothers, and sisters. These were years of real life and constant death. When I asked my mother about the concentration camps, she always said, "The ghetto was bad enough."

———

Eastern European Jews were often viewed from the outside as part of an undifferentiated mass, by both state officials and their own coreligionists in the West. And today, in light of our knowledge of their destruction, we tend to put them all in a single package, stamped with a number: so many starved, so many shot, so many gassed.

These observers miss the exquisitely intricate social structure that the Jews had created among themselves. This complexity among Polish-Russian Jews is often caricatured in portrayals of the conflict between Litvaks and Galizianers, a conflict situated in regional differences over religious beliefs and various social qualities; the Litvaks were viewed as more rational in religion and personally straightforward, and the Galizianers as more religiously enthusiastic and streetwise. In fact, centuries of Jewish survival was based in and produced a richly layered tradition of respect, social acknowledgment, prestige, and *yiches* (honor), a tradition hardly captured in this simple dichotomy, though its contours can sometimes be glimpsed in Jewish literature and folklore. The ways Jews judged themselves and each other could intersect with, but was never entirely congruent with, the ways they were judged from the outside, even when outsiders saw beyond the image of backward "huddled" masses.

Thus, outsiders might see uniform orthodoxy and religious traditionalism, as Jews addressed each other as "reb"—an honorific based on an assumed familiarity among all Jewish men with traditional Jewish liturgy. But Jews saw themselves along a spectrum of learning and ignorance that is sometimes glimpsed in the tales of the Jews from Chelm (ignoramuses). Moreover, Jews judged individuals according to their families, which could provide reflected glory on all family members from the achievement of one of them. Good families had learned members and encouraged that learning. This learning concerned Hebrew texts, not secular subjects, and distinguished those who could *daven* (pray) knowledgeably from those who could only babble (by heart) the basic and required prayers; those who could *daven* from those Talmudists who were seriously well acquainted with learned texts; those who could merely repeat those texts from those who had the wisdom and knowledge to interpret them. On this most basic aspect of Jewish life, Jews distinguished sharply among themselves. These distinctions might well also intersect with secular learning because often those marked as good at learning Talmud and other Hebrew subjects would also be likely to become good scholars in Latin and the medicine, law, and jurisprudence that was attached to its knowledge. Of course, they might not push in this direction because many Hasidim did not venture far outside their own *shtieblech*. Still, most of those who became acquainted with the Enlightenment ideas that had begun to penetrate the Jewish East by the late nineteenth century, in what is known as the Haskalah, were probably also well versed in Hebrew subjects. The ignorant tended to be broadly ignorant.

Of course, Jews judged each other by economic measures as well, and wealthy Jews were usually community leaders, and their families garnered various forms of respect. But these were not entirely unrelated to learning because only those who could afford it could allow their sons to proceed far into the hierarchy of Jewish learning (more rarely an unusually gifted boy received community support). It was not uncommon for families to buy themselves a scholar by investing in a poor but talented son-in-law. Thus, learning was by no means radically separated from social success. This intersection between social success and learning could also cross over into other kinds of secular achievements, as increasingly some secular knowledge of the world became necessary in a

modernizing world, either because of trade or because children were sent
to schools run by the state. (These could be designated Polish or Jewish
schools. My mother went to a Polish public school, though, when the class
was sent for religious instruction, she was sent for instruction in Hebrew
while others went to Catholic religious classes.) The wealthier Jews could
send their children to private Hebrew schools and academies; as a result,
they were often well versed in traditional Hebrew knowledge and also
became more successful in the economic world. The choice for Jewish
families, at least in the late nineteenth and early twentieth centuries, was
hardly one between being observant Jews or being secularly successful,
but usually both, and it was not uncommon that secular representatives
of Jews were also well versed in traditional textual knowledge.

The least well regarded in the Jewish community, those whose religious learning was minimal, usually had no other advantages either and
might well resent the hierarchy of learning because the learned were not
only more respectable but also wealthier, better connected, and more
powerful. Thus many nonlearned Jews were rapidly secularized, becoming outliers of the religious community. They might continue to live
exclusively among other Jews, if for no other reasons than their literacy
in only Yiddish and their unacceptability to those who were not Jews.
These poorer Jews would also have their hierarchies of self-respect as
they distinguished those who supported their families and led virtuous lives, something that became increasingly more difficult as Jewish
economic distress increased, from those who subsisted on charity and
handouts (*schnorrers*), from the growing underground of those who
lived outside the boundaries of respectability. An *urim man* (poor but
decent man) could expect occasional assistance from a benevolent community, which was always enjoined to assist the less fortunate and where
zdukah (charity) was an obligation and a blessing. Below them, by the
early twentieth century (though rarely discussed as part of the Jewish
experience), was a group of quite secular petty thieves, racketeers, pros-
titutes, and a generally rough element, still somewhat connected to the

poor virtuous Jews from whose ranks they had fallen. When Bibi and I were at the Yiddish theater in Warsaw, the performance centered on this less savory element, clearly a subject of self-reflection and commentary both within and outside the Jewish community. Increasingly then, being secular and being successful did not completely coincide. Certainly, in Poland, as elsewhere in Europe, successful assimilated Jews engaged in the professions or commerce. But it is a mistake to sharply divide the Eastern European Jewish community between the successful assimilated and the downtrodden pious; there were very wealthy pious Jews and very poor secular Jews.

It was doubtless among the poor, virtuous Jews whose lives were overrun with concerns about daily bread, not religion, that the majority of the followers of the many socialisms and Jewish nationalism (Zionism) that grew lushly by the turn of the century appeared, as seekers after justice looked toward either universal or more parochial solutions to the Jewish problem. These secular groups were often deeply enmeshed in a cultural *Yiddishkeit*, which drew upon the traditions of Jewish ideals of justice as well as Jewish habits, traditions, and rituals stripped of their God-centered piety and searching for some other belief. Socialism also drew from among the well-educated and prosperous children and grandchildren of the Jewish elite, some of whom were now going to the *gymnasium* and the university, where idealisms of all kinds flourished.

By the early twentieth century, these differences among Jews had left deep tracks in the texture of Jewish life in Lodz. While I knew little about my father's family I always associated them with the tracks left by the growing poverty of the masses and their secularization. Although they were deeply Jewish and certainly observant, following the laws of *kashrut* (keeping a kosher house) and abiding by the holiday calendar, his family members probably did not define themselves by their religious passion. My father was well versed in *Yiddishist* literature (a personal passion), but he disliked orthodoxy (including Hasidism) and distrusted most kinds of authority. His favorite authors were left leaning and highly critical of hierarchy and state power. He was deeply committed to matters relating to social justice though he was never a socialist. I always tell my friends that my parents would never have met, let alone married, before the war because they came from such different backgrounds and pasts. This is hard to convey to those who not only reduce all prewar Eastern European Jews to the ashes of history but also make rudimentary distinctions and assume that all Jews from Lodz were probably much alike.

My father's parents are mostly a mystery to me. Their photos were also in my parents' bedroom, but I knew less about them, and they played almost no part in my fantasy life. Because my mother either did not know his world or shunned it, she never discussed his parents and his family, except to say that they were very poor. (When she was in the hospital the year before she died and I was angry about something he did or said, she quietly told me that I needed to understand that my father was a simple man. She did not say *prost* meaning common, but *einfach* meaning straightforward and uncultured.) His parents were plain and honest people. That is all I knew. My father almost never discussed his parents with me.

The photos are of older people than those of Pola and Israel, a peculiarity of the historical preservation of documents, photos among them. And they seemed, as a result, much less romantic. My father's mother, *Sheindel Felzner Fass*, did not look like my father, or like me, and I could see little beyond the pleasant, open face and the modern summer dress with the white pointy collar. She wore her hair very simply away from her face, probably gathered in back into a bun. My grandfather had a trimmed, grizzled beard and looked a bit like my father but much sadder and greyer. I now know that these "portraits" were actually clipped (and enlarged) from a much larger family group photo taken sometime in the 1930s (see photograph). In the larger photo, my father's siblings (except one who was already in the Soviet Union with her family) and their spouses are portrayed, together with my grandparents, who are seated in front. They had gathered together in anticipation of the departure of

My grandparents, Sheindel Fass and Moshe Aaron Fass, seated in front with
a grandchild. Enlarged photos clipped from here of these two grandparents
hung side by side in our house. Also in this photograph are (in the rear), my
father's wife, Alta Isbicka Fass, my father, Chaim Harry Fass, Sarah (Srenza)
Margolit and her husband. In front, my father's sister, Rozia Fass, his brother
Yakov (Yankel), Sarah's son, Motel Margolit, my father's brother Schmul
Fass, and probably my father's cousin, Chana Fass. The photograph was
taken on the eve of the Margolit family's departure for Russia.

one of my father's sisters to Russia. By knowing today how close to the
war this picture was taken, I understand why these grandparents are
older and sadder. Even as a child, when I examined these Fass grandparents they looked much more careworn and, in contrast to my Sieradzki
grandparents, seemed not to expect much. Clearly not their poverty but
their life on the verge of disaster showed in their faces.

I was surprised to learn from the documents I collected in Poland
that my Fass grandmother, Sheindel, born June 4, 1883, was four years
younger than Pola (insofar as these birth certificates can be trusted).
Because my father and his sisters were older than my mother and her

brothers, Sheindel may have married earlier and/or had her children earlier. My grandmother Pola did, of course, lose two children before the three surviving children, so that might also account for the difference in ages. At the same time, it is difficult to know even how many children Sheindel had raised. I have never been able to identify (from records, memories, and pictures) more than six, although a cousin once told me that there had been ten. Did some of these die young? Did they all survive childhood? ("We never had impaired children," my father assured me, when I worried during my pregnancy. "They were always fully mature and healthy, no preemies or stillbirths.") Or did they just disappear from our memories because my father told me nothing about them and they left no trail? So many Jews disappeared this way, but I had hoped to save at least my family from this common fate.

Of the children I know about, my father was the second oldest and the oldest son, which might explain the discrepancy in the ages of the children in my mother's and father's families. My father's younger siblings (from the larger group picture of them I now have) were much younger, even younger than my mother and uncle Jerry. One of his brothers, my father told me, died at around thirteen (just after his Bar Mitzvah), on the operating table during an emergency appendectomy. My father dreaded "the knife" after that and was fortunate himself never to require surgery of any kind. This brother's name, might have been Yankel or Motel. And I also remember that he had another sister, *Reisel (Rozia)*, the youngest girl, whom he described as very vivacious. I knew nothing at all about others, although the photo I now have has another young brother in the group. My father always spoke these names with great sorrow and intense, barely concealed anger.

From my mother I know only two stories about my grandmother Scheindel. One time she slapped my father in the face, when he was already seventeen years old—fully grown and possibly already engaged to be married. The other relates to her generosity and extraordinarily kind treatment of the orphan cousin who came to live with them permanently when she was a small child. Both stories suggest a strong-willed woman, who kept control over her household.

It has always been difficult to imagine the poverty of my father's childhood, although my mother did tell me about her own in World War I Poland, when she went to bed hungry because the whole family had to share one heel of bread, and she was unable to attend school at one point because she had outgrown her shoes and they could not afford to buy her another pair. Both her knowledge of hunger and her lessons in shoelessness served her well later in Auschwitz and Bergen Belsen, when they had become her intimate companions. But her family's pre-Lodz ghetto poverty had been transient, not something inherent in the human condition. My father came from a family that had only poor times. He told me once that the very best place to sleep was "on the top of the stove," and I stared in amazement. He meant not the stove on which we cook today, but a large, tile covered hearth like those Bibi and I saw on our trip to Poland (and that can also be found in somewhat different forms in other northern countries, such as Sweden), still heating old museum rooms today. After seeing them, I understood why his favorite place to sleep (the place of honor) was "on the shelf." His poverty was bone-chilling and made an empty stomach colder still.

My father's family most likely had inherited its poverty, final descendents of a century of the increasing marginalization of Jews in the changing economy of Eastern Europe. The Jews and Poles had once lived parallel but separate lives. Jews were not part of the Polish peasantry with whom they traded in the shtetl economy. They were most certainly not part of the Polish nobility, for whom they had served for centuries as tax collectors, innkeepers, moneylenders, and, much less frequently over time, estate overseers. They were at the crossroads between these two firmly etched, almost castelike estates, but sharply separated from both; denigrated and despised by the aristocrats and suspected of exploitation by the peasantry, they had provided essential services that each group could not forgo.

During most of the nineteenth century, Jews were forced to endure the increasingly extreme Tsarist taxation and conscription policies, which pushed them further into their own secret world. At a time when Jews in Western Europe, after the Napoleonic reforms, were gradually invited into the civil community, the Russification of Poland drew Polish Jews further away from these possibilities, except for a small group of wealthy industrialists. Nicholas I's policy of mass conscription for twenty-five years (a duration true only for Jews) and the corresponding decision to enlist very young Jews (from eight to twelve) as *cantonists* (child trainees) created fear and loathing among the Jewish masses. The poorest Jews were most vulnerable because the wealthiest could receive exemptions, and, by using Jewish officials from the *Kahals* (Jewish self-governing bodies), Russification made the poorest classes of Jews ever more suspicious of all governments and leery even of their own Jewish officialdom on which Russian superiors depended.

The conscription policy helped to create a culture of deception among Jews, who misregistered the birthdates of their children or engaged in various forms of chicanery to avoid the horrors of conscription and the economic as well as personal loss to the family that this almost certainly entailed. My mother told me about young men who cut off their toes in order to avoid conscription or starved themselves until they were gaunt and feeble. This policy and the forced geographic separation of Jews by the restrictions on their residence to certain defined locations were never imposed to the same degree in Poland, but Poland's tutelage to Russia during the second half of the nineteenth century propelled many of the poorer Jews of Poland more firmly into their own separate worlds, walled in by distrust on both sides.

In the nineteenth century, Jewish economic life also changed because of the broad move toward industrialization that was transforming all of

Europe. As estates were dislodged, Jews were deprived of their former occupations, and throughout Eastern Europe non-Jewish locals began to develop their own middle class to compete with Jews in the commercial middlemen tasks that Jews had dominated for so long, such as trade in salt and liquor. Discriminatory legislation issued by the Russian tsars gave these new populations great advantages over the Jews. Increasingly, the Jews as religious outsiders, who had served important economic functions in a sharply divided feudal society, became economic outsiders as well. Some individual Jews succeeded in these circumstances through successful trade or industrial investment, but the masses were losing their roles and their moorings.

By the nineteenth century, autonomous Jewish life, as it had been for hundreds of years, was economically squeezed and politically defensive. Now Jewish outsider status had ever more stinging consequences. Jewish impoverishment, the existence of probably more than half the Jewish population on pipe dreams of small trade, resulted in new kinds of suspicions and separations. Jews were seen as *luftmenschen*, people of the air, without regular occupations, who had no standing and made no contributions to society. More and more Jewish families began to exist on whatever came their way: a little of this and a little of that, services within the community as matchmakers, occasional day jobs, or catch-as-catch-can services outside the community as dealers in various kinds of goods and merchandise. The poorest among them were described as "parasites" by the tsarist regime, which created a set of hierarchical occupational categories for Jews. Most Jews were classified in the lowest two groups, as "unproductive elements."

Increasingly then, Jews were viewed as "a problem," to both the societies in which they lived and their coreligionists in the West, recently liberated from their older pieties and seeking social integration, who began to devise charities that would deal with their situation. As the economic existence of the Jews of Eastern Europe became problematic, the life of a people who for so long had been outsiders because of perfidious religious beliefs and perceived insularity now became a problem of excruciating poverty for the masses of Jews.

The response to these economic transformations by Jews was not simple either economically or politically. A few Jews at the very top, those with access to capital or favors, grew wealthy by investing in the new railroads in Russia or the new manufacturing enterprises in developing cities like Lodz; some became professionals, although restrictions on enrollment in universities always kept this group very small. Jewish occupations diversified somewhat, as industry and crafts became more common. Some became artisans, tailors mostly, but also cobblers, jewelers, and furriers, though these kinds of jobs were not highly regarded among the people of the book. And the Jewish literature of the time, such as the stories of Mendele Moykher-Sforim, shows Jewish mothers wary of having their children learn to become laborers who worked with their hands. Many, like my mother's family, remained within their traditional occupations as small merchants and traders (in the terms set by Russia, merchants of the second rank); in newer cities, like Lodz, they capitalized on the growing prosperity and diversification of both the non-Jewish and Jewish populations.

My father's family apparently was less successful at maintaining their traditional form of livelihood, although my father clearly revitalized the pattern in his own life. And his own father was still described as a "Haendler" (tradesman) in the registry of the Lodz ghetto. I have always imagined that the origins of the name Fass (barrel in German) was somehow related to possible occupational identity among my ancestors, as liquor producers, dealers, or innkeepers. If my hunch is correct, then the liquor trade in which the Fasses may once have successfully engaged, also became far more competitive. The growth of non-Jewish competition and discrimination in innkeeping during the nineteenth century pushed Jews to the sidelines in an endeavor which they had dominated for centuries. Again, Russian legislation began to restrict this once dynamic Jewish form of enterprise. Many Jews were forced to live as day laborers—as porters, wagoners, or water carriers—or simply off charity, as the transformation of economic life and the continuing disabilities laid on Jews reshuffled the foundation of a previously stable society, making a few, such as Lodz's Poznanski family extremely rich, and most others, whatever their abilities or past prosperity, poorer and poorer.

By the late nineteenth and early twentieth centuries, Polish Jews were actively looking for alternatives to the economy of the shtetl and its centuries-old culture. Some, like members of my mother's family, including briefly my grandfather, Israel Sieradzki, traveled to the new world. Others moved to cities, like Lodz, where the textile industry was driving Poland forward into a new industrial age. Some emigrated to Europe, becoming known in Germany as *Ostjuden*, or England, where their poverty and habits often made their coreligionists ashamed and afraid. This seething and restless desire for improvement underlay both Jewish socialism and Zionism in Poland, other parts of Europe, and the United States.

Solutions to the complex problems faced by Jews came in many forms—socialism, Jewish nationalism, Polish nationalism, religious modernization, and an emphasis on cultural *Yiddishkeit* (Jewish identity). Initially defined in progressive circles in the late nineteenth century, these beliefs eventually moved beyond intellectual circles to affect the masses of Jews in Poland. Mendele, one of the first Jewish writers and a strong participant in the awakening of a new secular Jewish intellectual life, observed in his memoir that thousands of ordinary Jews, porters and draymen, greeted him on his tour of four Polish cities in 1906. Mendele, sometimes, known as the grandfather of Jewish literature, wrote about ordinary "little people" and the injustices they suffered, often at the hands of other Jews. Although he wrote in both Hebrew and Yiddish, he was increasingly identified with the literate Yiddishist strivings that became one expression of the Eastern European Haskalah (Awakening). He was addressing himself increasingly to a literate Yiddish-speaking culture; he was not among those who sought a return to Hebrew and with it to Zion, and he strove instead for social justice within existing Jewish communities. Their aim was not to assimilate, but to liberate Jews among themselves, an often deeply anticlerical and secular view. Mendele was one of my father's favorite writers. My father might have been one of those ordinary Jews who crowded around Mendele in Lodz (where he received an overwhelming reception) had he been old enough. Maybe my underemployed and Yiddish-speaking grandfather Moshe Aron was there to greet the famous author.

———

A French-Yiddish language film that Bibi and I saw at the Isaak Synagogue in Krakow (now a museum), made by the Baron de Hirsch Fund about the *Alliance Israelite Universelle*, showed the poverty of Galician Jews in the early twentieth century. It was to address this kind of poverty that the organized Jewish charities of much better-off Western Europe sent nurses and collected funds (hence the purpose of the film). Could the poverty of the Fass's have been so dire? The families in the film lived on the floor of a hovel (there seemed to be no furniture at all), and the children were left to grow like weeds on their own—with bad health, bad teeth, and uncombed hair. The nurses and schools established by the philanthropy sought to instill above all habits of hygiene, proper nourishment, and a nurturing attitude by the mothers, who seemed to be deeply ignorant but eager to learn. This film was about Galicia, and my fathers' family was from Poland. But how different could it have been?

This film viewed poverty from the outside, from the vantage of those keen to reform it and to hide the shame that it brought to the wealthy Jews of France and Germany. And I, as an American tourist, also initially viewed it this way. It reminded me of the immigrants to the United States at the same time. When people like these Eastern European Jews (maybe indeed some of these very people) came to the United States, they too became the objects of settlements, kindergartens, and visiting nurses. What the Alliance Israelite did in Poland, Americans of conscience, disgusted by what they saw descending upon the wharves of New York and Boston, did in the United States. But, in the United States finally and above all, these children went to school, something the Jewish poor of Poland early in the century (when Poland was still Russia or the northern outpost of the Austro-Hungarian Empire) were not forced to do or at least not forced to do for very long. It is hard to imagine such conditions today. It is harder still to imagine how children like these became the teachers and doctors of the next generation in America. In the United States they filled the City University of New York and a multitude of colleges at night and vied for places at Harvard and Columbia, which tried to cope with their tumultuous aspirations by imposing restrictive numerical quotas. But in Poland, they awaited a different fate: to join their sympathies to a socialist future through the Jewish Bund, to settle in the Soviet Union (as did my father's sisters), to emigrate to Israel in a dream of Zion (as did the sister of my mother's first husband), or to face Hitler's scythe.

It is unlikely (though not impossible) that the poverty of my Fass grandparents was quite so extreme. Certainly, seeing the Lodz ghetto made the reality of its poverty clearer to me. But, photos of the "old town" of Lodz, where the main Jewish district was located before the war, show considerable houses, not hovels. And while many structures were of wood and the district was more like a town than a great city, it seemed well-kept. This district had none of the manufacturing grandeur of the Jewish Manchester, as Lodz was called, but it did not look like the Galician Poland of the film either. Of course photographs are often taken to illustrate the best part of something, not the worst. And Balut was the least developed, and seedier. But my father always spoke about Balut with considerable fondness and humor, and he recalled his experiences there with warmth. No doubt most were extremely poor there, but not all were wretched and by the time my provider father was a teenager, he had been involved in business dealings for some time. He and his partner, Hainoch, were quite prosperous, or so my father implied. They traveled widely throughout Poland, where they traded goods and ate at restaurants and inns. Their poverty for the most part was not charity inducing, at least once my father developed his skills and his extraordinary capacity for hard work. Nevertheless, Balut was never a lovely environment. There were no underground sewers; it was close to marshy lands at the edge of the city, and the district contained both a Jewish cemetery within its environs (now gone) and abutted the large Jewish cemetery that still exists. An outskirt district, not fully integrated into prospering manufacturing Lodz where one-half of the large and medium-sized businesses were owned by Jews, Balut, even for those who eventually prospered like my father, was a badge of shame and hardly bound into modern European standards. From such districts and *stetlech* (little towns) throughout Poland and the "Russian Pale" of Jewish settlement in the late nineteenth and early twentieth century Jews fled to America to seek a better life.

My grandmother Sheindel and my grandfather Moshe Aron did not come to America. As far as I am aware, they, unlike my mother's family, had no relatives in the United States. They stayed in Lodz. They have no recorded *Anmeldung* at the Litzmannstadt ghetto because they already lived in that district of Lodz when the Nazis drove Jews from the better parts of the city and the surrounding towns to join them. They moved from the main artery of that part of town (a street later reserved for Aryans only) Limanowskiego, close-by to Masarska, which the Germans renamed Storchengasse. They were located in the smallest of the three segments into which the Nazis had divided the Litzmannstadt ghetto. In that, I suppose, they had the advantage because they experienced no profound shock in the relocation. But not advantage enough. My grandfather Moshe died there on August 10, 1941, hungry and sick with typhus. He had not yet reached his sixty-third birthday (born October 24, 1878). He died where he had lived most of his life. He may have been wheeled away as so much contaminated refuse. (There are pictures showing this process of disposal in the various books that now chronicle the life of the Lodz Ghetto.) My grandfather Israel died two years later, on June 5, 1943. He was almost sixty-three also (born November 23, 1880). But he has a grave somewhere in the Jewish cemetery in Lodz. I know this because my mother's cousin Basia, whose own grave Bibi and I found in Lodz, sent us a photograph of it. (I have recently discovered a photograph of my uncle and aunt at this grave taken while they were in Poland, immediately after the war.) Bibi and I sought out the grave site. I do not know if my grandfather Moshe was ever buried in a marked and separate plot. I hope so. Given my father's caretaking of his family, I think he probably was. I cannot believe that his plot went altogether unmarked; most photos show these vast graves in the Lodz ghetto marked with a small temporary paper placard. That paper cannot have lasted long. But I will continue to search among the headstones for both of my grandfathers in Lodz, where both had lived their lives in a city that never fully included them.

The record I have for Sheindel comes from the general ghetto registry taken in 1944, when she was still listed as alive in the Litzmannstadt ghetto, at "13 Storchengasse (Flat 7)." Her occupation is listed as a "hausfrau," just like my more ambitious and better educated grandmother Pola. When many of the fashionably dressed and educated German and Czech Jews, and the Jews from Luxembourg, and elsewhere in prosperous Western Europe who had been sent eastward to the Lodz ghetto were gone, starved or exterminated, my grandmother, Sheindel, who could not read, was still living where she had spent most of her life. She lived at this address with Chana Fass, my father's cousin. Chana is listed on the ghetto registry as a "waeschnaeh," a washerwoman. Chana was always hardworking. She had lived with my father's family, poor as they were, as their own child, ever since she was small and her mother had died. Chana always lauded my grandmother Sheindel, who treated her, she said, as lovingly as any mother, and she named one of her own daughters after her. Poverty was apparently no restriction on family feeling, generosity, or the sense of gratitude.

By 1944, my grandfather was gone, and so were my father's other siblings. Two (Brandel and Sarah) were in Russia, one had died on the operating table. Vivacious Reisl almost certainly went to Chelmno. The *Yiskor* (memorial) book of the Lodz Ghetto, which I saw at the U.S. Holocaust Museum in Washington, D.C., lists *Rozia Fass*, born on March 20, 1916. She was part of the first transport sent out of the ghetto and therefore almost certainly gassed in a truck and buried in the swelling ground. From the large group photo I now have, I found another brother, Shmulke, who was probably also taken to Chelmno. By putting together the picture of Shmulke in the family photo with the records of the Lodz ghetto, I was able to locate an *Abram Szmul*, born on May 5, 1922, and living at 13 Storchen (flat 7), the same address as my grandmother. At nineteen years old he was sent from the ghetto on July 4, 1941, to a labor camp, where he was either worked to death or sent to Chelmno, which began its operations in January 1942.

Those who survived the ghetto through to the end were taken to Auschwitz. Auschwitz came only after the years of starvation, the forced labor, the brutalized daily conditions, the beatings, the dirt, and the repeated selections in which loved ones disappeared, after the bitter cold and the graves with paper markings, after the typhus and the tuberculosis. My grandmother Sheindel and her niece Chana went to Auschwitz together. My mother went to Auschwitz with her mother Pola and with my mother's niece, *das einikle*. *Das einikl*, my uncle Avrum's daughter, my cousin *Chana Sieradski*, born on October 3, 1931 (almost certainly a reliable birthdate by that time) wore her long hair in braids wound around her head in order to look more grown up, my mother told me. She too had no doubt worked in the ghetto, but she did not make it. She was sent to the left with her grandmother, also my grandmother Pola, whom I knew only in my imagination. The selection was uncompromising for the elderly or those who appeared old and for the young, even those trying to look older. We knew of only one father, Harry Schweitzer, who survived the selection and the war together with both of his adolescent sons, a source of endless wonderment to my parents and extreme envy for my father. Neither of my grandmothers survived: one was already careworn before the war; the other certainly was worn down by it. None of the children survived. The Nazis hoped to get one last measure of labor out of those condemned to die, and they selected for hardiness and *arbeitfahigkeit* (ability to work). My father's cousin Chana had always worked hard; so had my father. Both Chana and my father came to America—he to New York, she to Denver. In Denver, Chana raised a family of three daughters, two of them bear names from the family in which she had been warmly embraced and whose names were thus not forgotten (Rosie and Shirley). These (and Linda) were the only American cousins I ever knew as a young child. In New York, my sister and I lived with our grandparents' names and our grandparents' photographs, but without grandparents.

CHAPTER 3

ONE UNCLE

Survivors are keenly aware of how diminished their families are. I was lucky. I had an extraordinary uncle, whose intelligence and character encircled my childhood and whose memory is an acute point from which I can trace my strongest commitments. My uncle Jerry never went to Auschwitz and never struggled through the experience of the Lodz ghetto. The youngest of the three surviving children in my mother's family, Judah in Hebrew, or Jerzy in Polish, was born in 1913. Unmarried and unattached when Hitler's troops occupied Lodz and its region in 1940, he was able to flee the city before leaving became impossible. In their secret 1939 pact that precipitated Germany's invasion of Poland, Stalin and Hitler had divided that country between them. Hitler got the western part, including Lodz, eventually incorporated into Germany proper, not just the greater Reich as was the case for most other areas of Poland that Hitler absorbed into his dreams of a greater German destiny. Soviet Russia was given dominion over chunks of Eastern Poland.

In the wake of the September 1st surprise attack that signaled the beginning of World War II, and as the sense of Jewish doom followed, many Polish Jews fled eastward into what had become part of the Soviet domain. There were communists and socialists among them, as many of the interwar generation of Jews tried to fashion new identities in the midst of a waning Jewish orthodoxy. But my uncle was not one of them. He did not think of Russia as a haven of aspiration. He was pragmatic: Stalin's Russia, unlike Hitler's Third Reich, did not take as its *raison d'etre* the complete elimination of the Jewish "race." My uncle became one of the tens of thousands who fled eastward during those chaotic days as it became clear that the Jewish situation in Poland, already seriously deteriorated during the 1930s as Poland's own turn to right-wing politics inflamed anti-Semitic beliefs and new legislation limited Jewish options, was about to get even worse. For those who kept up with the news, as my uncle always did, the danger was obvious; it was dangerous to go, but more dangerous to stay. Unlike German and Austrian Jews, and some wealthy Polish Jews who had earlier fled toward the West—to England and the Americas—most Polish Jews, without vast resources, fled to the East. And because he fled, he survived. He was my one and only uncle.

My uncle,[1] whom I learned to call Jerry in America, but who was otherwise known to my parents as Jeszik, was a remarkable young man. I always thought of him as young, and it became his fate to die young. As I write I see his face before me, with huge dark eyes, robust lips, and chestnut-colored hair. The pharmacist who occupied the corner store at the Carroll Street apartment house in Brooklyn, where I grew into my teens, identified him immediately as my uncle. There was certainly some physical resemblance between us, but the real kinship was deeper. My uncle was opinionated—he had strong views about almost everything, which he articulated with vigor and conviction. He taught me the value of such strong perspectives and the pleasures of passionate conversation just by observing him. And he taught me to value knowledge of all kinds—about geography, spelling, mathematics, the stock market, music (he loved George Gershwin and Tchaikovsky), clothes, and most of all politics. We would talk and argue for hours. Often when I was a child, he tested me on

---

1. Jerry Schiratzki—my uncle changed the spelling of Sieradzki in the United States. He did not change the name.

geography or math or history, not the stuff we learned at school, but things he thought I should know. He kept me very much on my intellectual toes. Although one of his most common retorts in conversations was "Sei nisht a kind" (don't act like a child), which he addressed to either child or adult, he rarely treated me as a mere child, but rather as a serious conversational partner. He also taught me tricks about calculations. My remarkable uncle was able to add, subtract, divide, and multiply quite large numbers in his head, very rapidly—something I could never do. Apparently both brothers and my mother were adept at this family trait. My mother would load her shopping cart at the grocery store and come within a cent or two of the final correct tally just before the cash register rang it up.

Uncle Jerry was very smart. But as the youngest son, it seemed to me, he had been forced to take a back seat to his brother *Abram (Avrum) Sieradzki* (October 9, 1908–April 1945), my mother's older brother. Everyone including my uncle Jerry agreed that Avrum was "a genius"—a man of truly unusual mental powers. He also had striking physical qualities, including elegance and great charm. Clearly the pride of the entire family, Avrum, even in his absence, became part of my life as a child because my mother and my uncle Jerry so often included him in their conversations as they reminisced about the past. From my mother's descriptions I pictured Avrum as very tall, but realistically I very much doubt it. Uncle Jerry was about 5 feet 5 inches; my mother was about 5 foot 1, which, she assured me, was tall for a woman of her generation. None of the Sieradzkis were tall, but they were all very smart, a quality giving them a certain stature that I must have translated, in the case of my never-seen uncle Avrum, into physical size.

My mother spent years after the war searching for Avrum.[2] In the months and then years after the Nazi defeat, the few remaining Jews of

2. When I examined the survivor's list for Lodz at the Holocaust Museum in Washington, D.C., I found both my uncle Jerry Sieradzki and Abram Sieradzki listed (RG-15-058, Reels 4 & 10). Of course, this may have been another person by the same name, but it would also account for my mother's belief that he might still be alive.

My mother's older brother, Abram (Avrum) Sieradzki, probably sometime in the 1920s.

continental Europe sought their relations by using Red Cross lists and interrogating anyone who might have any knowledge about an individual's whereabouts. This is how uncle Jerry found my mother after the war. My mother knew that Avrum had survived the initial selection at Auschwitz, and she learned from my father that he had been transported out of Auschwitz. My father met Avrum at the *reviere* (dispensary barrack) at Ahlem where my father worked and to which Avrum sometimes came because he was ill. Ahlem was one of the camps to which they, together with many other male Lodz survivors of the Auschwitz selection, had been sent after Auschwitz. My father did not yet have any personal association with him, but always contended that he was still alive just a day or so before their "liberation." My father could tell her no more. Others as well attested that he was alive when the Americans arrived. This near survival haunted my mother and offered just one more basis for the acute disappointment she felt about her loss of this wonderful and talented brother. All her life she dreamed that he might still be alive.

Avrum probably died just after he was finally liberated with the taste of freedom on his lips and the possibility of real nourishment close at hand, but neither available soon enough.[3] My mother grieved for him all her life, just as I grieve for her younger brother. I realize now, what I never did as a child (or took for granted as children often do) that Jerry's existence was a gift, that he could have disappeared like his brother to become a near survivor, hidden in a historical fold that now buries many other uncles. My mother's extreme solicitude toward this surviving brother is so much more poignant in this context as is my inability to comprehend, as a child, both her luck and mine in Jerry's survival.

————

Uncle Jerry gave me a lust for learning and a pride in its attainment. He was never shy intellectually, though he hated the showy (*schwitzers*) who bragged about their material success. He manifested a combination of tempered modesty and pride in his abilities appropriate to the family's respectability. Uncle Jerry followed my schooling carefully and was always proud of my academic achievements, though he often cautioned my mother not to exaggerate these lest I get a swelled head. He bought me my first English dictionary as soon as I started school. It was the first book in English I ever owned, though I have to admit that I did not use it as often as he would have liked and remained for most of my life a pretty weak speller. Uncle Jerry even influenced my parents' decision to move from 654 Lafayette Avenue in the Bedford-Stuyvesant section of Brooklyn, where we first lived, to 1040 Carroll Street, on the edge of Flatbush, not only because it was close to his apartment on Ocean Avenue but also because it meant I would therefore attend Erasmus Hall High

3.   Ahlem, outside of Hannover, was liberated by American soldiers on April 10, 1944. According to camp documents, "50–60 sick inmates" died in "Heidehaus," (the hospital) by April 12. My uncle, Abram Sieradski, was probably among these men. My thanks to my late colleague Gerald Feldman for his assistance in locating this information and to Douglas Greenberg of the USC Shoah Foundation for help in identifying the camp.

My uncle, Jerry Schiratzki in the late 1940s.

School. While he was attending night school there, he had learned that Erasmus was the very best school in Brooklyn, and he was eager that I have the advantages it could provide. My uncle, always knowledgeable about matters of this kind, had told me so much about Erasmus Hall's high standards that I was quite terrified when I started there as a sophomore in 1960.

Uncle Jerry's relation to my success must have been bittersweet for him. My uncle had preceded us to the United States and was initially an important resource for us in our transition. His English was far better than that of my parents, and he always read an English language newspaper. As I became an increasingly Americanized child, I began to replace his resources with my own. When I progressively succeeded at school and ascended in educational attainment I drew further away from my beloved uncle, and my contacts with him gradually shrank. He had less to teach me, and I had less time to learn from him. As a blossoming American, I was no doubt very full of myself and not so eager to be instructed. But my uncle did attend both my high school and college graduations. Although extra tickets were hard to come by (especially at crowded Erasmus Hall), I was extremely pleased to obtain

one for him. He heard my name often at the ceremonies as the honors
and awards were announced, and I can still picture his delight. After
my graduation from Barnard College, which involved a huge, open air
Columbia University commencement as well, we even had dinner at a
French restaurant in Manhattan, a once-in-a-lifetime event for my parents, who rarely indulged in such frivolities and never at a nonkosher
restaurant. My uncle was happy and proud that day but less excited
than I would have imagined. He was probably feeling the growing distance between teacher and pupil. He may already have been ill as well.

I recall getting his full attention as a child and spending some part
of every weekend with him. Jerry was kind and gentle, comfortable
with children and able to communicate with them—talents that went
largely unused because he had no children of his own. By the time we
had moved to East 27th Street in the Sheepshead Bay area while I was
an undergraduate at Barnard College (a distance that required my aunt
and uncle take a subway and bus to our house), I spent time with them
only on special occasions, and I almost never went to their house on
Ocean Avenue anymore. On the few occasions when I did go, it seemed
cramped and old-fashioned. I, who had loved the place as an exotic
haven of fine imported candy in an ornate dish (candy that was stored
in the beautiful old German sewing machine cabinet in their bedroom)
and elaborate powder, perfume, and hat pin holders my aunt kept on her
dresser, must have acted superior in my knowledge of American ways.
My uncle always considered himself more effectively assimilated than
my parents and more Americanized than most other "greeners" (refugees). If he was pained by my new pretense to superiority, he did not
show it, just as his kindness and courtesy prevented him from showing
this hurt to any other person. Without children of their own, however,
my uncle and aunt's lives had not evolved in ways that had been true for
my parents, who had to adapt to American children and their innova-
tive views on everything.

When I was in my teens and my uncle and aunt visited, they usually played cards (ten-card rummy) with my parents, and I was up in
my room studying or reading. Uncle Jerry never complained. He must
have assumed that I no longer needed him. Reflecting on this now, I
experience a deep pang of guilt and a sense of failure; I now know what
I had missed and would soon lose altogether. This doubleness (maybe
even tripleness) of emotion characterized my experience of the world
my parents brought with them as immigrant survivors. I knew that
their lives were special and precious because survivors were victims
who had almost died, holdovers of a now-dead past, and I was proud
of participating with them in that unique experience with the brutal
memories still clinging to everything they did. I realized also that my
uncle was unique, the sole survivor apart from my mother of a huge and
remarkable family. But a child also wants to separate from the cramped
perspectives this embodies, especially an Americanizing child for whom
thoughts of the future seemed to strain out all the restrictions of the
past. Even my "American" uncle, proud of his English and his ability to
adapt, inhabited another world. A good part of my experience was the
common inheritance of all immigrant children. And my uncle, with
his past untainted by either the Lodz ghetto or Auschwitz, was in many
ways an immigrant rather than someone who had risen out of the ashes
as my parents had. Jerry, however, had also experienced the excruciating
loss of parents and brother, and Hitler had stained his youth in ways that
marked his life as a survivor.

During that long painful process of my separating from their past, my
uncle was going through his own transitions and education, learning
to adjust to American habits and the different kinds of valuations such
adjustment required. Status in America was concerned above all with
money, not family or respectability, and less with education as a form
of self-development than as a means for economic self-promotion. This

value system was hard on him; he disliked the many *schwitzers* among his and my parents' friends who showed off their new prosperity in flashy ways and through loud talk. These people dressed in new fashions, added new layers of jewelry, and spoke loudly of their success. He must have felt that the things in which he felt pride had lost their value in this new environment.

My uncle, like my mother, had very good taste, the result probably of being the last of generations of independent traders and small merchants in luxury goods of all kinds on the Polish scene. They understood quality and could distinguish shoddy goods from those well made and refined. Probably their arithmetic ability (and the many tricks they learned to assist them in calculations) also came through generations of trade. Somehow, he agreed to discard that taste (it could hardly be forgotten) during the time he owned and ran the clothing store in Brownsville in the 1960s. He never brought us presents from the store, and, on the rare occasions when we visited him and my aunt there, he seemed somewhat abashed by the goods, which were perfectly decent. The store was large and well stocked (in a good corner location), but these were not the kind of goods we had learned to respect.

Before the war he had worked in a large, elegant stationary store on *ul* Piotrkowska and then on the same street in a men's haberdashery, where he was a sales representative with impeccable manners and excellent Polish. In 1930s Poland, such publicly visible white-collar jobs (*angestelte*) were highly regarded because they set their possessors apart from the ordinary workman and even the occasional catch-as-catch-can small trader in precarious times. It was a rare mark of status for a Polish Jew to hold such a post. With his polished nails and speech, my uncle's white collar and clean hands meant refinement in a Poland whose aristocratic past highly valued these marks of class. My mother once told me that as a young man my uncle, who never smoked (the only nonsmoker among the two couples), carried two cigarettes in a silver case to offer to others. The family never had quite enough money to send all the children to the

Jewish gymnasium, and there were many restrictions on Jews in the Polish public high school. As a result, neither my uncle nor my mother ever achieved what was in Polish terms "a higher education," by graduating from *gymnasium*, although Avrum had gone further than the other two because he apparently had some medical training.

Language skills they all had in abundance, however, and, because they were attuned to such things, my uncle spoke Polish very well. This was not true for many others, or so I was led to believe as a child, though I could not judge this independently, given my limited knowledge of Polish. My mother was immensely proud of the sound of the language she spoke—urbane, properly inflected and unaccented, partaking of a wide vocabulary that included many French touches (this from the aristocratic Polish past), words like *etagière* and *confiture*. My uncle and his wife always judged people by the quality and sound of the language they spoke. My grandmother Pola was literate in Russian, Polish, German, Hebrew, and Yiddish, and she often wrote love letters for other women who could not write for themselves. Maybe these language skills, too, were the result of the family's long history as merchants. My mother told me that during the First World War (a war which lasted into the 1920s as Poland and Russia fought each other) my grandmother sold goods to soldiers at the front until my grandfather forbade her to continue as he feared that a pretty young woman might encounter dangers in such circumstances. I presume she conducted business and chatted with the soldiers in their various languages.

Their facility with language went beyond the spoken word because they could also sing, something I badly envied, since I had inherited my father's tuneless voice. My mother's speaking voice was lyrical and fluid (as her good friend Jane Leon reminded me after my mother's funeral), and my uncle's singing voice sounded like velvet. He carried a little tuner with him so his pitch was always perfect. And he knew all the words, even of the English songs he learned in the United States. He often sang the words from songs on that popular 1950s television show, "Your Hit

Parade." And my uncle whistled brilliantly. One of the first things Uncle Jerry bought was a *pataphone* (record player) which he was always playing in their small apartment when we visited.

As soon as he and my aunt Fela arrived in the United States in 1949, they enrolled in night school so they could learn English, which they learned rapidly and well; they never needed a child to translate for them as my father did. They became citizens as soon as they could, not fearing the literacy test still required at the time. They voted immediately afterward. My aunt's English was almost without accent, perhaps because she had studied Latin in school, perhaps because she was eager to fit in. Like my uncle, she had been young and unmarried before the war, the third girl, the pampered youngest one, in a family from Czestochowa. My mother always suggested that my aunt inveigled my uncle into the marriage because he was (in my mother's view) clearly too good for her; she was shallow, vain, and self-absorbed. But my uncle and aunt seemed to love each other in that special way childless couples have, concentrat-

My uncle, Jerry Schiratzki, with my aunt, Fela Frajtag Schiratzki, just around the time of their marriage in Poland after the war (ca. 1947).

ing their attention on each other. They met in Lodz, to which each came after their different ordeals.

Fela was certainly pretty, with green eyes, an upturned small nose, excellent clear white skin, and black hair. She was five feet five inches tall, a very good height in those days for a woman. She claimed that she could pass for a Christian in prewar Poland, and she probably did. She also claimed that she could not speak Yiddish (to my knowledge, she did not have a Yiddish name), a claim that angered my mother who disputed this in private. Polish Jews, my mother insisted all knew some Yiddish even if they refused to admit it. I now know that in the region of Poland from which my aunt came, it was not that unusual to speak Polish rather than Yiddish. As a young girl striving for assimilation and the youngest in her family, she may well never have learned Yiddish or quickly left it behind early in life. Tante Fela always spoke to my uncle and my mother in Polish. This made things somewhat difficult for my father who neither liked nor spoke well that "foreign" tongue. Tante Fela spoke to me and to my sister in English, until much later when her diseased mind left her with nothing but Polish.

My uncle's life had been different than my father's both before and during the war. This wide divide cradled my understanding of the extraordinary and usually unacknowledged range of Jewish experience. Some of the sharp differences between my father's experience of Poland (and of life) and my uncle's were captured in an argument I overheard between the two of them when I was an adolescent. It concerned General Josef Pilsudski, the hero of the Polish Soviet War (1920–1921), and the man who presided over the first independent Polish state in a century and a half. Still remembered in Poland today, Pilsudski's birthday, as I discovered when I was in Warsaw, is marked by a changing of the guard. My uncle proclaimed that Pilsudski had provided Jews with real hopes for the future. He sought their integration into the Polish nation, tried to remove disabilities against them, and pointed the way to the new possibilities of a democratic nation. My uncle was still a youth when Pilsudski came to power in the middle of the 1920s and he identified with Poland and adopted its language. He apparently wanted to believe that he would have a place in Poland's future. My uncle wore a white collar and worked in an elegant shop on Lodz's main street; he was clean-shaven and tried, in his bearing and dress, to blend smoothly into the society around him. He spoke Polish fluently and well, and had Polish friends. The Polish nation might become his nation in the right circumstances.

My father was equally adamant that Pilsudski's was always a false hope, and his regime brought nothing new for the Jewish poor. He was quickly succeeded by a government of anti-Semitic thugs who imposed new disabilities on the Jews and brought nothing but harder and harder economic times and more discriminatory legislation. No, my father said, "the only real possibility for Jews was an empire like that of Franz Joseph" (the Austro-Hungarian emperor). My father, ten years older than my uncle, spoke Yiddish almost exclusively and grew up among other Jews. Because he had worked since he was a child, he had attended neither Russian nor Polish schools for very long. Although he too was clean-shaven and looked no more or less Jewish than my uncle, he thought Jews could never trust Poles and was looking for a model of Jewish semi-autonomy. He had neither faith not interest in assimilation into Polish nationality (and no interest in assimilating to American nationality either). He imagined a tolerant multicultural empire like Franz Joseph's might have offered the Jews such autonomy earlier in the century. Both my father and my uncle were Jews who sought to make a life and a living in Lodz before the Second World War, but they represented vastly different options for Jews, and their dispute suggested some sharply etched differences between my mother's and my father's sides of the family.

———

I cannot imagine growing up except in the presence of my uncle and aunt. Both were always part of my young life in the United States, where I situate my first memories of them. They brought us to the United States, although we were technically "sponsored" by someone else because they were not yet citizens. We might not have come here at all if my uncle had not preceded us in 1949. We had already sent a household of goods from Germany to Palestine-Israel, which was our original destination. I am an American today because my mother insisted on following her brother to the United States. When we arrived in January 1951, we stayed in their home for a short time, although we were officially at the Arlington Hotel in Manhattan (on West 25th Street), where the HIAS (Hebrew Immigrant Aid Society), paid our way. I remember spending one horrible night in their apartment on Ocean Avenue, the house with the liveried doorman (of which my aunt and uncle were very proud). I must have had a terrifying dream (just days after our arrival, or was it the very first night?) because I woke screaming in the dark and could not be quieted. My mother promised me all kinds of things if I would only stop, but I screamed for hours in the middle of the night and woke possibly everyone in the large apartment building (it had two cavernous wings). My parents were both alarmed and mortified. My hysteria was doubtless related to the strangeness of everything I was experiencing in a foreign place after a long and difficult voyage.

The apartment soon became familiar to me. When my sister, Iris Marsha, was born two and one half years later on May 30, 1953, I stayed with my aunt and uncle once again, this time by myself, while my mother was in the hospital (a full week in those days). Their apartment has been so imprinted in my mind, despite my many decades of absence from its premises, that I can still sketch it in great detail. Its windows faced onto a side street (on which we could see a subway exit though you could see the park from the bedroom). We reached this small but always very neat and tidy apartment on the fourth floor of the left-hand side of the building by an elevator attended by an operator (the first I had ever seen) who manually closed its huge brass accordion-pleated grate. I even remember the small closet with its very special coal smell near the backstairs with its loud trap door where we brought the trash. The building at 115 Ocean Avenue was directly across from Prospect Park, with its many attractions, including a small zoo, ice skating rink, bandstand, concert shell, and boat house.

In this building on Ocean Avenue we also met the American-born Feldmans (Howard and Anita, I remember, because I often helped my mother address her Jewish New Year cards). This kindly and wealthy older childless couple were fond of my uncle and aunt and friendly toward me. They may have helped my uncle and aunt in their acculturation process. Mr. Feldman asked me to call him "Uncle" Howard and gave me an old silver dollar from his collection (my first object from the 1920s) and a jade elephant, both of which I still have. In their living room, they had an assortment of beautiful puppets, including a copy of the famous Howdy Doody puppet. I never knew why the puppets were there, but I could always play quietly with these while my parents visited. My parents expected me to be well behaved in their house, and I related this to the fact that the Feldman's were childless, but it may also have been related to their impeccable American credentials. Never a rowdy or restless child, I was easy to persuade to stay quiet, but at the time I associated these carefully controlled manners with my uncle and polite Americans. The last time I saw the Feldmans they were living in Spring Valley, in upstate New York, and were "in retirement," but as far as I can remember neither of them ever worked; they either inherited money or lived on the fruits of shrewd investments.

My uncle always worked in a store; he was either an employee in a men's clothing store or the proprietor of the store he and my aunt owned and ran for many years. He always took a proper summer vacation, which my mother tried to insist that my father do as well, though she was not usually successful. Thus, my uncle and aunt would join us when we went "to the country" in the summertime. Starting from the time I was eight and my sister was two, my father rented a cottage for us in a bungalow colony in the Catskills. Before long, I claimed to have outgrown the experience and refused to go. While we vacationed in the Catskills, however, my father ventured out on a spring weekend to find a bungalow for us; he rented the "best" bungalow he could find in the particular locale chosen by the group with whom we regularly spent the summer, people with pasts like that of my parents and with children my own age. We had known many of them in Hannover, Germany, before we came, and we all arrived in the United States at more or less the same time, within a year of each other. These friends were always known to me as "oncle" and "tante" a kind of pretend family that made us feel less alone. After a few years, we were also joined at these places by my father's business partner, Bernard Wietschner and his family, even though they were Russian Jews (Litwaks) and had not shared the Polish experience of ghettos and camps. During these summers, our group recreated some facsimile of the lives we had lived in Germany, and the air was rich with stories and memories as well as the laughter of children and the conviviality of summers. Many of these people became quite successful in the United States, and we continued to know about each other even if we no longer met in any regular way. Almost all of them were younger than my parents.

There was a real hierarchy among and within these cottages as some locations rated higher or lower in the scale; prices varied accordingly. Those locations further away (close to Monticello) were more inaccessible and less expensive. We never owned a car (my father insisted that he was too nervous to drive) so that the closer locations were a necessity because my father commuted back to New York City on Sunday night after arriving late Friday evening and spending the weekend with us "in the country." Bernie Wietschner drove us up to the country with our goods bundled into his car. After my father's partner joined the group of country vacationers, my father rode with him on Fridays and Sunday nights, but before that he commuted by bus. Over the course of years, we moved steadily upward in the quality of our bungalows; our final location, a place we had heard about for years, was especially choice and a sign of our prosperity. As the places became better so, too, it seemed to me, did the adolescent boys, my primary preoccupation, become more and more attractive. The cottages never had a telephone, and our summer sojourn meant a real break from ordinary time and place, an adventure into a freedom that was clearly revitalizing to my parents.

Our very first bungalow colony—near Monroe, New York, and close to New York City—was largely peopled by refugees like us. Although it ranked low, it was also the most memorable. Instead of a blue chlorinated pool, it had a lake for swimming, and the whole place tended to flood, as the back fishing lake and the front swimming lake joined their waters after heavy summer rains. Each of the two years we stayed there we had to be "rescued" by rowboat from our cottage in order to stay overnight in the hotel on the high ground of the premises. I found these floods exciting, but my mother was in despair as we returned to our wet rooms afterward, rooms to which she had brought her sterling silver tableware and Rosenthal china in those first summers in the country, much to her later regret. She always prayed that my uncle and aunt not be scheduled to come when it flooded.

Although we rarely had more than two (and later three) rooms (one of these a kitchen-living room combination with a sleeper sofa) plus a screened porch, my mother always found room for my uncle and aunt who came up for a week and sometimes two. Usually, she gave up her own and my father's double bed as the rest of us made do with an assortment of ad hoc arrangements. (My father never much liked the whole thing.) During that time, she cooked elaborate meals for my uncle and catered to his needs. She seemed somewhat resentful of my aunt's princess status as a guest but enjoyed being able to please him. And my uncle loved it, exuding a sense of relaxed vitality that I can still feel in my memories of him dressed in a white tee shirt, light-weight summer trousers or shorts, and brown leather sandals.

My uncle, as the youngest son, had probably neglected the family's orthodox Judaism even before the war. By the 1920s many children of the orthodox were taking deep steps in the direction of assimilation, and, according to my mother, the younger generation was often in open rebellion. Some, she told me, made a point of eating ham sandwiches on Yom Kippur, intentionally scandalizing community standards. The modernization of the Jews of Eastern Europe was in full swing, and, as the youngest child in an orthodox family, Uncle Jerry must have felt that pull. Uncle Jerry kept his views about religion largely to himself. In the United States, my uncle never went to religious services, did not own a *talit* (prayer shawl), and did not even go the synagogue on the High Holy Days, which my mother always regretted and often noted. I suspect that he did go to *Yiskor* (the mourning service) on Yom Kippur, but I never saw him go, he never said he went, and my mother only assumed that he did. He always, however, came to Passover at our house.

Passover was an eight-day ritual, carefully observed at our house with two special sets of Passover dishes (marking the traditional separation between meat and milk as well as the separation from non-Passover food) as well as pots and silverware. The house was scrupulously prepared, and no *chumetz* (non-Passover food) was allowed in the house—neither food left from before Passover nor that introduced during the holiday. The two kinds of foods and the dishes in which they were served, as well as the pots and pans for cooking, could not mix. As a child, I remember well that I passed up the most tempting Easter candy during this season when I visited the homes of many of my Jewish friends. My mother cooked traditional foods: chopping and cooking her own gefilte fish, making matzo ball soup, baking sponge cakes and potato kugles, and preparing every other variety of delicious food. The most pleasurable part and the highlight of the celebration was, of course, the two evening seders on the first days to which my aunt and uncle always came and through which they sat while my father read the entire service in Hebrew, every word, from start to finish. Toward the end of the evening, my uncle sang the *"Chad Gadya"* (One Kid, one only Kid) beautifully. One Passover they brought us a decanter and a set of matched etched glasses, which even today remind me of our Passovers. And they always brought a box of specially designated Passover chocolates or a can of Barton's molasses chews. Passover, my favorite of all the

Jewish holidays, was the most genuinely warm and embracing. My uncle and aunt also came on Thanksgiving, the American festival most easily adopted by my immigrant parents. Turkey, cranberries, stuffing, and yams quickly became a part of my mother's repertoire, since these were easily absorbed into the kosher kitchen but also because the symbolism of the holiday—gratitude, family, and historical survival—made sense in our circumstances.

I loved Uncle Jerry very much in all his details. He had a scar below his left eye that made it droop, the result of a wound that he received when a guard's ring struck him (before or after he left Poland?). As a result, his eyes were never quite symmetrical. He also had a deformed index fingernail (injured in another similar mishap). And I loved the gold signet ring that he wore on the pinky of his right hand (and which, initials now completely effaced, I have kept). He spent the war years going further and further East, out to central Russia, Kazakhstan, and possibly well beyond, into deep central Asia, an area about which we in the United States are just beginning to learn. He said that he wandered in snows up to his waist in places on the Russian Steppes, places where no one had been before him, which I doubt, and lived on huge squashes (*banyas*) as his sole source of food for weeks and months at a time, which I can believe. The local population treated him well and shared whatever they had with him. He was a nice, nonthreatening person. I never heard him raise his voice or utter an obscenity. He may also have lived at some point in a Soviet labor camp as many Jewish refugees did, although he never told me this, and, to my shame, I never bothered to ask. He may well have avoided doing so because the family had probably sent along with him whatever resources they could spare so he could survive in a strange place amidst the chaos of wartime.

After the war, he went back to Poland, back to Lodz, where the family had lived, to find no one. He managed to somehow locate in the ghetto and retrieve the few prewar family photos that we now possess. No doubt he and the family had corresponded, and he knew their address. No photos showed him as a boy, but the photos are the only physical connection I have to my grandparents and that time and place. He also erected the double monument to my grandparents that Bibi and I failed to find. As a child, my uncle had given me so much, even the resources for my fantasies, although he could not have known this. In Poland, he met my aunt Fela, to which she too had returned, but from enslavement in a concentration camp (*katzet*) not the snowy ranges of Asia, and they married soon after.

———

His eating habits were always problematic, maybe because of those banyas on the Russian Steppes or maybe from being the youngest child. He never ate much, and his tastes were well defined—no tomatoes ever, very fresh bread and butter, and mostly bland, carefully prepared food. He developed a taste for American steak that he cooked himself, once a week, in a huge broiler that stood in their kitchen like a loved and carefully tended object, but all objects were carefully tended in that house where no child disturbed them. My aunt was a good enough cook, but it was my mother's cooking that he especially loved. From a young age she had begun to cook for the family in Lodz. And my mother, I think, loved to cook for my uncle because it gave her a sense of a past of which she had been otherwise deprived, a taste of home so to speak. When he was really sick, during his last few weeks, she went to his house every day to cook for him, trying to coax some appetite with the delicate foods of childhood, like whipped eggs twirled in hot chicken soup, and other things that were light and nourishing.

My uncle, like my mother, suffered from digestive problems. Both had gall bladder disease; he had his removed when he was fifty, and I remember visiting him in the hospital where he seemed terribly pale and small. Then, when he was fifty-four, the doctor found colon cancer during a routine exam, and his life was never the same again. The word cancer was rarely spoken in my house, and then only in a whisper, as if by naming it was invited in. Everyone assumed it was a sentence of death.

That sentence was forestalled for almost five years in my uncle's case. With the help of friends I made as a graduate student in the late 1960s, we found an excellent surgeon at Mt. Sinai Hospital, and I called and made an appointment for my uncle. He had a large private room at what was then considered the best private hospital in New York, where my mother had also had surgery, and the doctor told us after the operation that "the cancer had been successfully and completely removed. With luck, he should recover completely." He left the hospital with a colostomy bag.

He was never completely comfortable sitting after that, and he was conscious of the bulky device. This must have been especially galling to my intensely fastidious uncle. His squeamish eating habits worsened. My mother would fuss and fret, and my aunt's life was redefined as she became the person responsible for caring for him (until then he had always been the one who took care of her). And now he had elaborate personal bodily needs. Uncle Jerry who was always youthful tried to seem lively, but the natural vitality and good spirits were gone. They talked a lot about health and how important this seemingly natural fact could be to a person's luck and fate. He was smaller, and his eyes became less symmetrical. His color was hardly ever really good. Although the colon cancer supposedly did not recur, everything else seemed to attach itself to the delicate site—first prostate problems, twice treated, and then cancer in the kidney. Because everything was hushed, I never knew if this was a new cancer or the site for the spread of the original. In either case, he had not gone cancer-free for five years. He seemed resigned, and I never heard him complain throughout the ordeal. The sense of the tragedy of survival now haunted my parents as the approach of his death became a reminder of the remainders of death that always clung to their lives.

By then I was so removed from his life that I would not have bothered to notice. Our paths had been moving apart for years; his own bright promise as my "Americanizing" uncle had shrunk, and my own

Americanization, initially under his tutelage, forced me forward by using the language and the history of the country to which my uncle Jerry had led us. He watched me go there but only so far.

The last time I saw him was in New Jersey. I had moved to a small suburban garden apartment complex near New Brunswick shortly after I began to teach at Rutgers University in 1972. I was eager to have him come to my new adult home and to cook for him, having somehow taken over my mother's role rather than the role of the student-niece. My repertoire was as limited as were his tastes, but I remembered past meals he had enjoyed so I decided to cook turkey. My mother warned me that he might not eat at all and that he was having a terrible time sitting. But he came. My sister's husband Jeffrey drove all the members of my family in his huge old Plymouth Fury— my mother, father, uncle, aunt, and sister—out across the two bridges from Brooklyn to New Jersey. And Uncle Jerry ate. To my surprise and joy he told me it was very good. Ever since, I have prided myself on my ability to cook turkey.

My uncle died on December 18, 1973. I was finishing the last chapter of my dissertation, the chapter on student politics in the 1920s, during Christmas break. I would soon defend it officially at Columbia. I was in my own home in New Jersey, having just completed the first semester of my second year teaching American history at Rutgers. My mother, as always, wanted to give me the space and freedom to work. She had done this since I was a child. She never told me he was dying. When she called to tell me he had died, I was enraged—enraged by the news, enraged by her failure to give me a chance to say goodbye, enraged by my selfish self-absorption. That moment of recognition is now deeply burned in my memory. My uncle was dead. My life had changed forever: the dissertation was finished; I had my first adult job; and my uncle, my one and only uncle, the companion of my childhood, the best teacher I ever had, was gone. Two years earlier, I had lost another cherished teacher, Richard Hofstadter, and still felt bruised.

Jerzy, my mother observed with sadness, "had not made it to sixty." I cannot remember the funeral or anything about the *shiva* (seven-day ritual period of mourning), which I buried in my rage. What remained was my mother's loss and mine. My mother had lost almost ten pounds during his dying, and she was never the same again, having lost her younger brother, the last part of her past, the part hidden in the Russian Steppes to stay alive. Now only she was left. And I had lost my childhood.

CHAPTER 4

THE COMPLEXITY
OF AUNTS

As a child in postwar Germany, I had many aunts—Tante Edja and Tante Bella, Tante Bronka and Tante Henja.[1] All my mother's friends in Hannover, where we lived as people removed from history, were *tantes* (aunts) to me. They were all from somewhere else, all fleeing memories of the day before. I called them *tante* out of respect (just as I learned to curtsy) because they were adults and because we were very close, having created life anew with each other. But I knew even then that we were not related, that the kin group we created was connected by the similarities of experience, not blood. And I knew that our relationship grew from real need.

We eventually settled in New York City in the early 1950s; some lived in the Bronx, we, in Brooklyn, to be closer to my uncle. We saw each other regularly—at first, almost every weekend, and daily during the summers in the country; later, we gathered only for special occasions. I continued to call them all *tante* throughout my childhood and even when I grew up. And one of them, Tante Bella, moved within a block of my parents' house in Sheepshead Bay where they confirmed their friendship and I got to know her quite well. Four of these *tantes* came to my wedding, though my mother was no longer alive. Although they rarely visited my father or spoke on the telephone with him after her death, they came to

1. Edja (Esther) Jakubowitz, Bella Koss, Bronka (Betty) Prywes, Henja (Enid) Henson.

my wedding because they were still my father's friends and because they remembered when we had all been together in Hannover. We still needed one another because we now shared a past created during that sojourn in Germany, a past from which they had spun out a new future. That future grew from a leap of desire rather than either reason or hope.

Women friends my mother made in the United States did not become *tantes* to me, even if they had backgrounds like ours. And just as I very quickly learned not to curtsy here, I learned not to adopt every friendly woman to the status of aunt. In the United States I also learned that I had other kinds of aunts, "real" *tantes*. These, it turned out, came in multiple and complicated varieties. These included my Tante Fela who was closer to me than Tante Bella or Tante Edja because she was married to my Uncle Jerry, though like these other *tantes* she was not technically related to me. (Years later, when Tante Fela was suffering from Alzheimer's disease, my sister protected herself from fears about inheriting the disease by declaring emphatically that Fela was "not blood.") There was also my mother's American aunt, Tante Toby (Toby Weill), whom we went to see very shortly after we arrived in the United States. Finally, my father's two sisters, *Brandel Fass Rosenzweig* and *Srenza (Sarah) Fass Margolit*, were unlike my uncle, and not only because there was only one of him and several of them or because they lived far away and I saw them infrequently. My uncle always remained special, even heroic, to me, but my aunts were more complicated, like most other human beings. Above all, my aunts allowed me to reflect on the human and unpredictable as well as the grim reality of surviving.

———

Tante *Toby Nawry Weill* was very important to my mother because she was her last connection to the previous generation, a connection to which she clung literally until the day when Toby died. After visiting her every day at the hospital to which she was taken after her heart attack, my mother went to visit her once more only to find the bed empty. She returned home in tears.

Tante Toby was one of my grandmother Pola's younger sisters (she had ten), and my mother had never known her in Poland because Toby came to the United States early in the century, before my mother was born. Despite this, my mother and her aunt would chat as if they had never been out of each other's lives; they recollected family stories and peopled their talk with individuals known only to each other. Toby came to America to be a bride and a replacement for another of Pola's sisters (whose name I never knew) who had married a man named Weill. This sister had borne a son, my mother's cousin, Walter, and then died either in childbirth or soon thereafter. It was apparently customary among Eastern European Jews when one sister died, for the husband to summon another to replace her, especially if there were some advantage to the match. As it happened, Pola had many sisters, all born in the last quarter of the nineteenth century. My grandmother, as the oldest, was responsible for all of them after her own mother, Blima, died (in childbirth or soon thereafter). They had come from Wyszogrod outside Warsaw, but by the late nineteenth century they apparently were all in Lodz. Mr. Weill decided that he would replace his dead wife with Toby Nawry. My mother pointed out to me that rather than several of the older sisters who were still unmarried and available Mr. Weill had chosen the young and appealing Toby. Pretty, blond, with lovely grey-blue eyes, and a pretty singing voice, Toby was a desirable replacement, even though her husband was considerably older. She had obviously caught Mr. Weill's attention even as he married her older sister, and he remembered her after crossing the Atlantic with his first wife. Her good looks and cheerfulness earned her a trip across that ocean to a new world that saved her from the fate of the other sisters and the rest of the family.

When Toby came to the United States as a designated Jewish bride and replacement for an older sister, she was given the opportunity to escape the narrow life of Jewish Poland, but it was hardly an easy life to which she came early in the century. She came young and pretty but prepared to be Walter's stepmother as well as his aunt. In turn, she bore Mr. Weill two more sons, Max and Morris. In the manner of the American dream, her family was destined for wealth and renown. In the meantime, her husband toiled as so many immigrants toiled on the Lower East Side of Manhattan and eked out a living. Burdensome as it was, toil in America was both more fruitful and more hopeful than in Poland, and the Weills invited my grandfather, Israel Sieradzki, to join them in this work. So Israel came to America, to the Jewish American haven of the Lower East Side, the original entrepôt of burgeoning Jewish wealth in America. My grandfather stayed briefly, probably no more than a year or two, before returning to Poland at the beginning of one war, only to die in the next. Because her father had stayed with the Weills, my mother considered that she had ties to Tante Toby through both her mother and her father, and, in her mind, these formed a knot of intimate family memory.

My memories are also secure though less fervent. When we met Tante Toby she was already long widowed and living in the Bensonhurst section of Brooklyn in a small but always impeccably kept apartment. The hallway of the apartment, between the living room and Toby's glass-doored bedroom, was dominated by two large portraits of members of her Polish family: one was of my uncle Avrum (of whom everyone in the family on both sides of the Atlantic was clearly very proud). We have a similar, but much smaller, picture—one of those few rescued from Poland by my uncle Jerry after the war. (See photograph in chapter 3.) The other portrait (I believe) showed Toby's (and my grandmother Pola's) only brother, the youngest of the Nawry children who became a wealthy Polish stocking manufacturer. In the portrait, he wore a mustache (I think), but no beard, and modern dress. (No doubt there were other family photos on that wall, but I remember only these.) In this uncle's country house, large and full of servants, my mother sometimes spent several weeks in the summers, a place where she may have learned the finer points of table setting with silver utensils and embroidered linen that she displayed when we had guests at our house.

Toby's Bensonhurst apartment was the only place in which I ever saw Tante Toby because she never came to visit us. I can still vividly remember being picked up and escorted by her youngest son, Morris, in his beautiful, shiny, black, chrome-encrusted Cadillac, with its creaky leather seats. Morris, still a bachelor and living in Toby's apartment, was kind and charming. As far as I can remember, we never met Max, the other son, who had by then settled with his family in Texas. Texas seemed like another country to us, but there his family began its rise into the American stratosphere of wealth. Toby always told us, with her eyes rolling upward, that "Max was very rich," having invested well in Texas's burgeoning economy. But it was Max's son, my second cousin, Sanford Weill, who later became a familiar name and face to me as one of America's great financiers and philanthropists. I have seen him on the cover of innumerable magazines and frequently interviewed on television and in the *New York Times*. As the organizer and founding genius of City Group, and benefactor of Cornell Medical School and Carnegie Hall, Sanford Weill has become the personification of the American success story. Physically, he closely resembles his grandmother Toby, especially in his grey eyes and nose. Sanford Weill and I have never met.

My Tante Toby and my mother sat in Toby's kitchen for hours talking about the old days. Although Tante Toby spoke English quite well (inflected with a Yiddish accent), they always spoke with each other in Yiddish. My mother was Toby's connection to a lost world, much as Toby was my mother's link to a previous generation. They genuinely liked each other, though I knew from the time I was very young that my mother's American cousins, Toby's children, kept their distance from us, possibly because we were greenhorns at a time they were rapidly becoming Americans or possibly because they feared that, as recent refugees, we might expect or need assistance from them and become a financial burden. It was not clear immediately after the war when the remnants from Eastern Europe were coming to the United States that they would, for the most part, prosper and their children become well schooled and highly successful. Only Walter, Toby's stepson/nephew was in regular communication with my mother. (Was he perhaps born in Poland himself? I do not remember.) Despite this distance from the cousins, my mother loved Toby and grieved for her deeply after she died. After the funeral, which neither my father nor I attended, my mother told me that the "American cousins" kept to themselves. "They were at the other side and were not interested in Jerry or me." Only with Walter did she have any subsequent connection. I believe that he even came to my uncle's funeral, although I have no independent memory of this because I can remember nothing about that event.

The fate of Toby and her children and grandchildren, from hard work to success, and from success to great wealth was the American parallel to my grandmother Pola's story. She too had had great expectations, but Poland's hard times gave way to death and destruction while America's hard times gave way to something altogether different. My mother, the link between these two stories, must often have reflected on this parallel, and she may have also thought about the different fate of her wealthy industrialist uncle who has left no historical trace (none that I have been able to find) and the wealth of her cousin (though she did not know of his son's extraordinary achievements when she died) which led to great success.

———

Between Tante Fela, a real *tante* but not related by blood, and Tante Toby, related by blood but a great aunt, and my several fictive *tantes*, one might have thought that the complexity of aunts had been exhausted, but this turned out not to be the case. When I was about seven years old, I discovered that I had other kinds of aunts, real relations who lived in another country on another continent. Not only spatial distance but also a distance in age separated me from them, for these *tantes* were closer to Tante Toby's generation than they were to the aunts other children had or my aunt Fela. I discovered the world of these aunts when my cousin Bella Rosenzweig came to visit from Israel in the mid-1950s.

Bella was already in her mid-twenties when I was seven, but she was lively and pretty. She had come to meet, and possibly to marry, a man who became fascinated by her beautiful photograph. Once she met him, she knew that she would never marry him, but she stayed for quite a while in the United States—first with us in Brooklyn, and then in Denver with my father's cousin Chana and her family, and after that she never entirely left. She did marry, a much more interesting, younger, and far more important man than the one who had been dazzled by her photograph. She was introduced to Rabbi Richard Hirsch while she was in Denver; the summer camp where he was to serve as rabbi was searching for a nurse. My cousin Bella was trained as a nurse, and during the summer in this camp their relationship bloomed. As soon as I met her, I was fascinated by this "cousin." She had all the glamor of unmarried youth. As a child, I was entranced by her and bewildered by the new confusion of relationship—by a cousin who was so much closer in age to a conventional aunt and by new knowledge about her mother, an aunt who could have been my grandmother. Indeed, this tante's daughters had children who were my age.

Bella, I learned, was my Tante Brandel's youngest daughter, and the only one of the three daughters still unmarried (there was an even younger son named Chaim). Bella was born in Russia where my aunt spent the war. Tante Brandel was the oldest of my father's siblings. My father, the next oldest, was the only surviving son. A whole new world opened to me as the many aunts and uncles destroyed by the Hitler devil were joined now by a few individuals who had survived.

With my cousin Bella's arrival in America, I learned for the first time that my father had *two surviving sisters*, very much alive, and I had two real *tantes*. They had survived the war in the East, like my uncle Jerry. It was now clear that Russia offered real possibilities of survival, not just isolated instances like my uncle. In Russia my aunts had managed not only to survive themselves but also to keep their children alive. This was very unlike my father's fate in Poland, where his children had all been destroyed.

In this manner I learned for the first time that my father had children before the war and that they too, had they survived, would have been grown-ups like my cousin Bella. My mother told me about my father's children, with some reluctance but undisguised grief; she made it clear that this territory was not to be encroached upon with my father. The generational displacement and confusion over aunts and cousins stemmed from the fact that we (my sister, still a baby at the time, my mother, and I) were my father's *second* family, and quite a bit younger than the first. Thus, my cousin Bella's arrival marked a distinctly new chapter in my life.

I had always known about my mother's son, but I thought of him as a dead brother. I had given little consideration to her husband and never before thought of us as a second family. But with the discovery of this new paternal set of siblings and the very full family they had formed, including children who were cousins to my lively cousin Bella, my mind was asked to absorb another whole dimension of historical facts. I was confused, disturbed, and intrigued. My father had never spoken about these children, and my fascination with my father's lost family, begun in this initial discovery, has remained with me ever since. The details of who they were, how they were lost, details never provided by my father, have remained obscure and dangerous edges of a history I can never fully penetrate.

———

When we originally planned to go to Palestine, it was apparently to join my father's sisters, and we had shipped an entire well-stocked household of goods (including luxury items, such as a grand piano and a car) to Israel. These had been sent to Tante Brandel (Bella's mother) who, as the oldest of the two surviving sisters, was entrusted with their care. After it was decided that we would immigrate to the United States, not Palestine, she was supposed to distribute the proceeds of their sale between the two sisters. But Tante Sarah, my father's other Israeli sister, contended that she had received nothing at all, while Brandel had kept all the goods and the money from their sale to purchase a fine apartment for herself in Ramat Gan, just outside Tel Aviv. Brandel assured my father that she had not profited from these goods and that the apartment was to be my father's when he came to Israel. As a result, whenever my father was disappointed with my behavior or that of my sister Iris (whom we always called Marsha as a child), he told us point-blank, "I can leave at any time and go to Israel where I already have an apartment and where my nieces will take care of me." This illusion lasted only until the first time he went to Israel, and the fiction was completely dispelled by the second trip. But it worked to keep us in line when we were young because my father could disappear to this alternative place with all its resonances of a previous (preferred) life where he could expect greater respect and gratitude than his American children would provide. In this way, I always associated my father's sisters and his nieces and nephews with his far away first family. While he never spoke about his lost family, his potential for escaping to Israel was a deeply painful reminder of this other life.

In Israel, in the meantime, Tante Sarah (also known as Srenza) never forgave Brandel who, she believed, had benefited from the sale of expensive goods during extremely hard times, while leaving Sarah and her two sons stranded. Neither sister had a husband to support her; the men had disappeared in Russia. But Sarah spent a lifetime working as a cook in a cafeteria and living in a rented apartment, while Brandel never worked at all and lived in the apartment apparently paid for by my father's goods. (In fact, Brandel was supported by her deeply devoted children who cherished and cared for her in old age and whose son visited her every day to wish her good night.) As a result of this feud, Brandel and Sarah did not speak to each other. Like so many resentments, this one was inherited and carried forward into the next generation. My Israeli cousins, children of Sarah and Brandel, rarely speak to each other, and only see each other at family events. (See photograph on p. 96, taken some time in the very early 1950s, of the two Israeli aunts seated together.)

This feud was the very first thing that I remembered about my two
aunts. It left an indelible impression when I visited Israel in 1967, after
the Six Day War, when my family fought its own war over me. I had been
traveling in Europe during June and July (a graduation present from my
parents after college) and then expected to travel from Rome to Tel Aviv
by chartered plane. My transportation turned out to be cheap, but not
fast. Because of the recent war, Israel insisted on transporting all visitors
on their own planes, and Israel had few planes or pilots to spare. My
charter therefore landed in Nicosia, Cyprus, where all one hundred of
the passengers waited for a small crate-like Israeli prop plane to pick us
up and take us to Lod Airport. That plane could carry only twenty passengers at a time, and my group was the last. That one little Israeli plane
therefore flew back and forth four times before picking up my group.
Although Cypress is not far from Israel, my flight was delayed by almost
sixteen hours.

Both sides of my father's family were at Lod Airport: Brandel's side
and Sarah's side, glowering at each other as they waited for me. Each
had sent three delegates. Not one of the three people on one side spoke
to anyone on the other. Only one side could capture the prize. Eventually, they would have to share me during my stay, but initially, at least, I
could only go with either my Tante Sarah or with my Tante Brandel. As
usual, Brandel won. "Where were you," my cousin Shoshanna Bronstein
(Brandel's oldest daughter) yelled, "how could you be so late?" Tired,
nervous, and upset about the long delay during which time I had no
way to let my family know about the circumstances (long before cell
phones), I was immediately put on the defensive. But Shoshanna, in a
good imitation of her mother's manner, got her prize, and I was carted
off to stay with her in Hadera, a city on Israel's northern coast. Shoshanna's husband had quickly grabbed my luggage, and I had to leave
a crestfallen Tante Sarah and my other cousins while promising to see
them all later. Whenever I think of my aunts, I remember this event, but
the feud was well known to me before I landed in Israel. That it showed

no sign of resolution or even of temporary cessation while I was there signaled its intensity and duration.

This is how I will always think of them: two sisters who wound up in Israel together, after the devastation of Poland, the hell of Russia, war-after-war for Israeli survival, two sisters who could not communicate at all. Maybe they can now commune with each other in death. They died a year apart, at the end of the twentieth century, in the land of Israel. Both had survived my father. Brandel, the eldest, sat *shiva* for her younger sister, Sarah, with whom she had not spoken for decades.

After her daughter, Bella, had married and settled here, Tante Brandel came to America. She came to the Port of New York on a ship from Israel sometime in the 1950s. At a dock in Brooklyn I met my first "real" Tante. Her curly thick hair (like my father's and mine) was a wonderful mix of grey and black (my father's was still quite black). She was about five feet three inches tall, but appeared taller because she always wore high heels (usually sling-back, open-toed shoes). She closely resembled my father, except that she was far more self-possessed and imperious.

My aunt had learned the habit of command when she was left stranded in a Siberian camp with four children and only her own resolve and determination for support (although I think its roots must go back to her childhood). Apparently, she had been left alone in 1937 when her husband was arrested by Stalin's police and accused of being implicated in one or another plot that haunted Stalin's mind. We never spoke of this, except in whispers, since Tante Brandel all her life did not know what had become of him. She, her husband, and the two oldest children, left Lodz quite a while before the war and were in Russia when the war broke out. It was never entirely clear to me how important Brandel's husband had been in Polish leftist politics before the war, but he had clearly found it useful (or perhaps necessary in the Polish political climate) to go to the Soviet Union. It is now clear from a document that my cousin Bella has sent me that he, like so many others, was innocent of the charges, but he was shot anyway, shortly after his arrest. There was little room for innocence in Stalin's Russia, especially among Polish Jewish socialists whose beliefs were assumed not to be entirely trustworthy. Left alone with her four children, my Tante Brandel never knew his fate after his arrest. When she left Russia after the end of the war, reluctantly following her daughters and two sons-in-law to Israel, she must have felt either that she was abandoning him or that he had abandoned her. Left in limbo, Brandel suffered not only from her husband's absence in war torn Russia where she had to support her family on her own but also from an indifferent state that left her an uninformed widow. My other aunt's husband was also a leftist, and Sarah had left Poland with her husband and young son to follow the older sister around 1932. Sarah and her sons knew that he had been recruited into the Soviet army where he was killed as a soldier. His fate was clear.

The husbands of these two aunts were *never* openly discussed. But I do remember my mother suggesting that it was a great shame that these two attractive women had never remarried and remained alone for the rest of their lives. Sarah, quite a bit younger than Brandel, had been clearly widowed. Brandel's situation was, of course, much murkier. Russia had been their salvation from the Holocaust nightmare, but neither Tante

My aunts, Brandel Fass
Rosenzweig (left) and Sarah
Fass Margolit (right), together
at a family event in the 1950s.

Brandel nor Tante Sarah, though survivors, had been left unsinged by its flames.

Brandel came to the United States many times after that first passage by ocean-liner, sometimes staying for several months, always staying with us for a part of that time even after her daughter Bella had settled permanently in a lovely colonial house in Bethesda, Maryland, where she raised four children. In the meantime, Bella's husband became the director of the Religious Action Center of the Union of American Hebrew Congregations, an expression of reformed Judaism's and Dick Hirsch's engagement with the civil rights activism of the 1960s. Tante Brandel rarely brought us presents of her own, except for chocolates, though she was often the conduit of presents from our cousins, or from Mrs. Gros, my mother's former sister-in-law, who lived in the ultra-orthodox area of Bnei Brak. This was my mother's one (distant) connection with Israel. My Tante Brandel always expected to leave laden with goods, especially electrical appliances which she purchased for herself or her children. She also loved to buy crystal, porcelain, jewelry (mostly costume), and clothing of all varieties and in many sizes. Some of these things she received as gifts from us or from our cousins in Denver; some even came from my mother's friend and close neighbor Jane Leon. During her stay, she always expected my mother to take her shopping, repeatedly haunting appliance stores that sold exportable goods (with the right AC current), department stores, bric-à-brac stores, stores that sold china and housewares; she spent the first weeks scouting and the remainder buying goods. My mother was always worn out by these shopping excursions. Things needed to be sent in advance, or they needed to be properly packed and the right suitcases acquired. By the time Tante Brandel left, always from New York, she did so accompanied by bulging suitcases that usually tipped the scales of what was permitted for international travel. She had spent days packing these, so that everything would fit in. New York was her mecca, and she stayed with us partly to visit but also very much to shop.

By the last two times she came to visit us, my mother was tired of it all (and tired out by my uncle's illness), and my aunt, now older and beginning to tire herself, began to shop on her own, going by herself on the subway, always in her high heels even when she was well into her seventies and when there was snow on the ground (at which times she wore high-heeled boots). That she could do this on her own was quite remarkable. Unlike my father, who read voraciously and constantly in Yiddish, both books and newspapers, and could read some English very slowly and deliberately, my aunt's literacy was more problematic. She apparently never went to school in Poland, or in Russia, or in Israel, and she was, as a result, without the skills to read even subway signs; she learned to count the number of stops so she could locate the proper station (I remember my mother instructing her in this). I do not know whether she could read or write numbers, at which my businessman father was a master. Therefore, the act of shopping on her own, of maneuvering in the vastness of the New York City subway system and its multiple lines, or getting cash register receipts (let alone trusting that they were accurate) was something of a miracle.

But then, my aunt had managed to raise, house, feed, clothe, and school four children through decades in Russia in the most deplorable conditions, and she had safely shepherded them to Israel so there was little that she could not master. Indeed, her will and her determination were quite extraordinary. Without access to written language she had willed herself through three continents, by train, boat, foot, and eventually by plane (long before either of my parents had flown and before most of her own children had). She had mastered primitive as well as modern forms of transportation, many forms of money, and she had retained a kind of sovereign power over her children, all four of whom loved, honored, and obeyed her. "Respect," she often repeated to me, "has to be earned; it cannot be taken for granted, even from children." By this she implied that my mother had not earned it because she was too weak and compliant. She died when she was almost ninety nine, a strong woman who had endured very tough times.

Tante Sarah (Srenza) was not like her, in either looks or character. She was short and heavy where Brandel was always svelte, even in old age. (Brandel kept an eagle eye on her diet, sometimes by eating mostly lettuce hearts and lemon juice.) Sarah was white-haired since her youth, according to my father. When I stayed with her in Israel, she had made sure that I always had a plate of grapes in front of me because she was concerned that I was too thin. Gentler, more generous, and more cheerful, Tante Sarah's face was unclouded by the imminent disapproval that sometimes shadowed my Tante Brandel's beautiful features. Sarah looked Mongolian, with her wide, high-cheek-boned face and narrow long lips (something like the photo I have of my father's mother). Her hair was straight and long, and Tante Sarah wound it first around her hand and then around her head. She had neither her older sister's self-possession nor her mental agility. She, no doubt, suffered from the comparison which Brandel never let her forget.

By the time I met her, when Sarah too came to the United States and visited with us (not to be outdone by her sister), she repeated the same story three or four times and suffered from what seemed to be spells of memory loss during which she blanked out for several moments as she stared out the window or into space. She also suffered from terrible headaches (all of them did—my father, both sisters, and many of their children). Like her sister, she brought us presents, among them watches, and hand-wrought gold bangle bracelets that I still wear, and she seemed more genuinely grateful for whatever she was given, whether these were material gifts or gifts of affection and concern. She rarely went shopping, but mostly sat in the house, happy to just be with us, cheerful rather than lively. She too had endured terrible times in Russia and had, by herself, brought her two sons out of Russia through postwar Poland and Germany, to the land of Israel, where she single-handedly raised and supported them. One son, Motel, a genuine intellectual with whom I discussed Hegel when I visited in 1967, took me to intellectual cafes around Tel Aviv. Trained as an engineer, he had invented a new box configuration and as a result always made a respectable living. The other son, Yankel, was extraordinarily handsome, both in his early photos and when I met him later in life; he resembled my father somewhat, but with flirtatious green eyes. Yankel, who drove an Eged bus most of his life, has since died of lung cancer, the first of my cousins to die.

When Sarah's husband went to Russia early in the 1930s, he took his young bride and their son Motel with him. (See photograph of my father, his parents and his siblings taken on the occasion of their leaving, p. 49.) He, too, had leftist sentiments. They probably left Poland as a result of the increasing rightward tilt of politics and almost certainly because of the bad economic times of the 1930s. Whatever his beliefs, these could not protect him from the deadly wartime conscription of the able-bodied in Russia, a society fully engaged in war by 1940. His sons worshiped Stalin in the late 1940s when they came through Germany on their way to Palestine-Israel. My mother remembered going to Tante Sarah's tiny room, almost completely filled by an iron bed and whose remaining floor space was covered with their books. Motel was lying on the bed and listening to a Russian radio broadcast of one of Stalin's speeches. Throughout, he would punctuate it with loud exclamations of "Stalinov," "Stalinov." Whatever had been his other experiences in the Soviet Union, he had clearly been well schooled in loyalty to both the Soviet state and its leader.

Regardless of her husband or her children's political and intellectual aspirations, my aunt Sarah, like Brandel, was bereft of the ability to communicate beyond the spoken word. My father's parents seemed to have made few efforts to educate their older children in a secular way; most likely they simply could not afford to send them to school. The sons had been given access to Hebrew *heder* and therefore to Jewish literacy. The prewar Lodz ghetto, the "Balut" of my father's fond remembrance, had formed its inhabitants along lines that had translated poverty into educational neglect and linguistic disability, and it had deprived girls of access to the written word. The government had apparently overlooked them or considered them too insignificant to bother with. The ghetto girls married young (Brandel before eighteen), raised children, cooked and kept their homes kosher, lit candles on Friday night and at the beginning of all the holidays, and thus fulfilled their religious obligations (from generation to generation). The last time I spoke to my Tante Brandel on the telephone, just a few months before she died, she reminded me, not unkindly, that I had been an old maid, but that in the end I had redeemed myself by marrying and having children. All the Fasses had resources—good looks, will power, and shrewd intelligence—but the refinements of the book and the pen were strangers to most of the generation that had grown up even before Hitler had come to rob them. Whenever my mother wrote to them in Israel (she spent one evening each week at the task), the letters were sent to one of the children (all literate and educated in the Soviet Union) who read them aloud to my aunts.

Imagine, therefore, the strained interaction among my three "real" aunts—Fela, Brandel, and Sarah. Brandel and Sarah never talked to each other, though they lived a few blocks apart in the Tel Aviv suburbs. They made sure never to come to the United States at the same time. And when they visited us in the United States, neither could speak with Tante Fela, who had been educated in *gymnasium* and was fluent in English, German, and Polish and had even learned some Latin. Fela claimed to speak no Yiddish as a child, and the others could speak nothing else (though both in time did learn to speak Hebrew, and Tante Brandel even learned some English). Over the years, my Tante Fela learned to speak Yiddish, hesitatingly but clearly; she was obviously gifted in languages. And she did occasionally speak with these other aunts when they visited, but never more than a few words. They had nothing really to say to each other, even though they had come from the same country and each had been a victim of Hitler. Tante Fela had no children, while Tante Brandel and Tante Sarah really had few other things to talk about. Brandel loved to shop, but my aunt Fela's shopping was largely functional. She would have liked to discuss books she was reading. They greeted each other politely, but never spent any time in each other's company. They all had been in Poland before the war, but these real aunts might have come from different worlds. They would not have known each other in Poland, and they hardly knew each other when they met in the United States.

I loved both Tante Brandel and Tante Sarah, and not just out of obligation. They were both colorful, and Tante Brandel was intense and queenly, while Tante Sarah was warm and sweet. My feelings about Tante Fela were much more complex. I cannot imagine my life without her, but she was married to the uncle I adored, and I could never quite divest myself of the idea that she was not of his caliber, well educated but not really intelligent; I may have simply absorbed my mother's prejudice. While my uncle never showed anger or resentment, she was labile and had explosive emotions, which were easily ignited. As a child, I used to love to stand in front of her large dresser mirror and try out her many hat pins, powder, and perfumes. But, if she caught me she would erupt in anger. My mother instructed me always to be very careful with the things in her house, and this dedication to delicacy did not inspire affection in a child. She insisted on her autonomy and denied her dependence, but she was childlike and fragile, much like her porcelain (and well-powdered) beauty. Later in life I felt extremely sorry for her and protective: sorry for her childlessness, for her aloneness (she hung around with us but only as a hanger-on), and for the loss of her youth.

Felicia (Fela) Frajtak Schiratzki[2] had been the youngest of three girls, still a child she insisted, when Hitler bound the fate of the Jews of Czestochowa to his vision of a cleaner future. Known for its shrine to the "Black Madonna" and Catholic inspiration, Czestochowa was a

---

2.   My uncle and aunt changed the spelling of Sieradzki in the United States. They did not change the name.

My Tante Fela Schiratzki, around 1950.

small city, some miles north of Krakow, in a region where Polish had become the dominant language even among Jews. Although my mother was skeptical, it was certainly possible that my young aunt knew very little Yiddish. It was also possible (though my mother did not believe this either) that she had been born in 1920. This would have made her only nineteen when she was robbed of the bright future to which she probably felt entitled as a very pretty, well-educated, and pampered young Jewish woman, who looked like a Gentile and was eager for assimilation in one of the more progressive regions of Poland. I never knew or discovered when she went to Auschwitz or how she survived there or at the camps to which she was subsequently sent, but I could imagine that her young life was distorted beyond repair, just as her back would eventually be irreparably bent out of shape.

When I first met her she had a tiny waist, the smallest I had ever seen, and the most kinky black hair. As she aged, the slight curvature of the spine, a deformation that was hardly visible earlier when she was young and thin (and with which she was probably born), took over her body. The years of working in the camps and then in the United States—first in a chocolate factory, and then with my uncle at his store—must have

also taken their toll on her back. By the time she was fifty, she was
severely crippled and forced to walk with a cane. That crippling of her
body, complicated by severe arthritis, progressed rapidly. The last time I
saw her walk alone outdoors followed my mother's death when she had
come to attend our *shiva;* it looked like the top part of her body was at
a right angle to the bottom. She soldiered by herself to the apartment in
Sheepshead Bay where she, like my parents, now lived. The sight of her
walking was heart-wrenching. When I later accompanied her to do her
banking, she leaned heavily into me to maintain her balance while caus-
ing me considerable discomfort.

In her mid-fifties, in addition to her crippled back, her mind began
to give out. She would stand in the hallway of the garden apartment
complex where she lived and scream at passersby that she was being
persecuted. "They are all Nazis. Stop the Nazis. They are beating me
with chains." She believed fervently that the people in the apartment
above hers were trying to whip her with thick metal chains they kept
under their beds and with which they beat the floor above her every
night. She could not sleep. By then, my mother had died, and Tante Fela
was terrified and felt herself to be alone. Her paranoid fantasies became
increasingly problematic for herself, her innocent neighbors, and us.
The landlord was concerned about the disturbance she was making and
often called my father or my sister and her husband in Manhattan to
complain. He asked for advice, but they had none to offer. We tried to
calm Tante Fela's fears, but now that she was really and truly alone—
with my uncle dead and my mother dead—she seemed to be sliding into
some nightmare of the past. My father, who visited her regularly (as in
all things my mother had been provident in this, too, by bringing her
from Ocean Avenue to within walking distance of our house) found her
always alone in a house that was scrupulously clean and dead. No one
called her any more. She, who had had a few well-chosen friends and had
once read voraciously, now sat for hours by herself, not comprehending
and reading the same paragraph over and over again. Occasionally she

watched the television flicker, but most often she simply sat by herself in the dark. My father walked past her apartment in the evening to check on her, and it was usually dark.

Finally, my father concluded that it was time for my aunt to go to Israel, where her surviving sister and a handsome nephew lived. My father made all the arrangements, packed up her things, and took her to the bank so she could forward her funds. To do this was no easy task because she leaned into him while walking very slowly, one bent step at a time. He helped her to sell all my uncle's stocks, although it was the worst possible time for the stock market. My uncle had thousands of shares of Chrysler, which were now valued below two dollars a share as the company slid toward bankruptcy. But this seemed hardly relevant to her now. Her Israeli brother-in-law came to escort her, and they flew to Israel to join her sister.

Now, all my "real" aunts were very far away. When I got married on July 13, 1980, none of them came to my wedding. My uncle and my mother were dead. In their place, were my four fictive aunts, Tante Bella, Tante Edja, Tante Bronka, and Tante Henya, my mother's friends from Hannover. Several of my cousins came as a delegation from Israel and also attended, but not my cousin Bella.

It never worked out in Israel for my Tante Fela. Her sister probably had no idea how bad her back really was (she could no longer walk on her own) or the extent of her mental deterioration. And my Tante Fela had never, even at her best, been easy to care for, always insisting that she not be treated as a dependent child. Her sister, she wrote me, tried to treat her "like a baby." We wrote letters to each other on thin blue aerograms. Within a couple of months she asked to be "rescued." "I miss you very much," she said. "I miss speaking my own language," by which she meant English. She could speak no Hebrew, but it was more than language that upset her. She did not feel at home. Finally, she called my father. And my father, who had always thought of my Polish-speaking Tante Fela as haughty and disdainful of him, went to Israel to bring her home.

He flew to Israel alone. This was only the second time he, who was afraid to fly, had ever been on an airplane. The first time he had gone with my mother who had guided him. He did not stay in the apartment he had long believed was his. He was not treated with unusual gratitude by his Israeli family. He came back with my crippled aunt, whom he then settled into his own new apartment by putting her and her things into the larger master bedroom while he took the small narrow one. It was truly an astonishing turn of events. Now neither of them was alone, and a Tante had become what she had been from the beginning—someone you needed in adversity and who needed you.

Their household was odd, to say the least, because her Alzheimer's was progressing through its awful stages. Fearing that she would cause a fire and "burn us both down," he could not trust her to cook. He would not leave her for long and would not dream of traveling outside the small neighborhood perimeter. She sat, and he served all her needs. My father, who had never lifted a hand in our house, where my mother did all the housework while he was the provider, now shopped, cooked, washed dishes, cleaned. And Tante Fela, trusting no one, became progressively more withdrawn. She kept her jewelry, wrapped in a handkerchief, on her person at all times, When she needed to go to the bank, she insisted that my father take her, and they would walk together slowly, she leaning her full weight into my father's chest. She never allowed him to deal with her affairs. I don't know if they ever talked much. Although he claimed that she drove him crazy with her nonsense and that he could not travel as a result, the arrangement somehow lasted until he died. I wonder if he did not use that odd living arrangement as a shield to protect him from the women who eyed my handsome father and often came calling right after my mother died. He had always been kinder and gentler than he admitted and she far more dependent, but no one could have ever predicted that he would wind up taking care of her.

When my father died ("It didn't take long," she assured me, as she apparently watched and did nothing to help), my husband and I brought Tante Fela to Berkeley, California. My husband, Jack, spent several weeks on the telephone while we were in New York making arrangements to put her in a nursing home near us in the San Francisco Bay area. It was required that she be examined by two doctors: one in Brooklyn to assess her mental state, and one in Berkeley for a physical evaluation. She resisted both. My own personal physician, Norman Cohen, could not examine her because she would not let him near her, and she would not undress. He was reluctant to sign papers about an exam he could not complete. She did not want to go into the nursing home; instead, she wanted to stay with us.

Initially, Tante Fela had ample funds to make her a desirable patient (the home charged outrageous amounts each year), but finally her money ran out. She stayed in the nursing home for eight years. My daughter remembers her vaguely, and even my son Charlie remembers when we used to visit her at the home, although we never took them with us to see her. I felt that it was enough, that Hitler had inflicted his toll on too many of those who survived and their descendants; too many had witnessed the breaking lives of those who had been lucky enough to survive. I wanted to offer at least some protection to the next generation. Tante Fela spoke nothing but Polish by this time, and even Jack, who always came with me to see her, could not understand her. My mother had clearly been wrong about her because Fela reverted to the language she learned as a child.

By the last two years of her life, she was entirely bedridden and could not speak at all; she communicated only by gestures with her terribly bent hands (she who had always condemned those who spoke with their hands). She may have had a stroke, though her doctor seemed unsure of this. She had also had hip replacement, but the home was never clear about how she had broken her hip. Her body and her mind were both damaged by the war and had been further destroyed by its aftereffects. She was young when she became ill and probably no more than seventy when she died. We took Charlie to see her that night, and he remembers seeing my dead and finally peaceful aunt. Some things, like death, cannot be hidden. After a small service at our synagogue, I arranged to have her coffin sent back to Brooklyn, to be buried alongside my Uncle Jerry. This had been her one request when we brought her out to the West Coast. She had insisted, and we had promised, that she and Jerry would lie side by side; she would no longer be alone.

My aunt was the only one of the four people who created my childhood to be alive when both my children had become part of my life, although she hardly knew this and they scarcely knew her. During the time that I knew her, she had been taken care of by me and by all the people I loved—my uncle Jerry, my mother, my father, and Jack. She was my most essential aunt.

CHAPTER 5

FIRST FAMILIES

So saith the Lord: "One hears a voice complaining and a bitter crying on high." Rachel cries over her children, for it is over with them.

—*Jeremiah* 31:15

The past was everywhere in my childhood creating memory tracks. There was the picture no one ever saw and the names no one ever uttered. These were the secret realities that lay behind the everyday in my house as I grew up. These unseen images and unspoken words haunted our lives—dead children, dead spouses, even more awful than grandparents who were unknown and unmet. Grandparents died, after all, even American grandparents, and my mother, too, had never known hers even without Hitler's help. But no one I ever went to school with had siblings who had died. And what were the dead husband and dead wife of your parents called? Were they stepparents once removed, almost parents? Hidden behind everything we were and almost everything we did was an earlier life, only partly lived, of which we were either the afterward or the substantiation, or possibly the redemption, but without which our consciousness was incomplete. The abbreviation of earlier lives made ours possible, and I was both eager to compensate and bewitched by the past from which my own identity was cast forth. The injured past conceived me and coughed me up. I knew that this same past would have consumed me or could never have produced me at all. This unpredictable vulnerability gave me, from my earliest days, a sense of history. "What happened to those children," I asked my mother when I was not yet three? "They were taken away." "Will they take me away too?" I wanted to know. I learned soon that the answer was a matter of luck, and a matter of history.

How do you write about them, people who were at once all important and always there, but never part of my life—people who had *no names*? My grandparents had pictures and my parents lit *yahrzeit* (memorial) candles in their memory. And my sister and I bore their names, spiritual reincarnations according to *Ashkenazi* Jewish tradition. But I was never even told my mother's husband's name or that of my father's wife. Only when I went to Poland, years after my parents had died, did I learn the names of these nameless ghosts. *Zaynwel Kopel Kromolowski* was married to my mother before the war. He was born on September 18, 1908, and died in the Lodz ghetto on May 8, 1943. I know this only because, many years after my first childhood lessons about the past, I became a historian and found the records: first a birth certificate for my mother's son and the name of her son's father with the other birth details.

Only once did she talk about him, though she did regularly write to his surviving sister in Israel, a sister who had settled in Palestine well before the war in an expression of Zionist yearning and a prescient instinct for survival. Out of respect for their religious piety I wore long sleeves and a long skirt when I visited them in Bnei Brak in 1967. I always knew her as Mrs. Gros. These "relations" sent us news about their children and photographs. They wrote to us of their successful matings and of their grandchildren. They shared their lives with us and sent us gifts. And my mother always kept the tie, sending them gifts in turn. When my mother was extremely ill, we let them know, and they put a request for her recovery into a niche in the Western Wall (a *kvitl*) and asked the "great rabbi" in whom they still believed for divine intercession on her behalf.

She had married very well, into a rabbinic family that was very highly regarded in certain circles, although her husband made shoes in the Lodz ghetto. When my mother once mentioned the name of his parents to a counterman at a dairy on DeKalb Avenue in Brooklyn, where we regularly shopped, he stopped what he was doing and made a point of acknowledging the standing of the family. This was *yiches* (prestige and honor). She always had that, my mother, a knowledge of the *yiches*, even after she lost her son. He was taken, along with the other sons and daughters, during that horrible week in the Lodz ghetto when all the young children disappeared. On September 4, 1942, the Jews of Lodz were ordered to give over their young children. During the following eight days in what was called the "*Gehsperre*," the ghetto's children, together with many of the sick and elderly (those over sixty-five) were transported to their deaths in truck caravans.[1] She sent him off with a piece of bread for the journey placed in a little sack around his neck, which she had sewn. I learned this only very recently from my cousin Bella and her husband, Richard Hirsch. From the documents I know now that less than a year after that, she also lost her husband. My mother never talked about either loss. She only wanted daughters she told me, and as a child I assumed it was because she liked girls best. She, after all, loved dolls and played with them, not me. Now, with children of my own, I know better. Each child's identity is precious and distinct. No doubt, she could not face having another son. In this one thing, her wishes came true. In her second family, she had two daughters.

1. Here is one description of the events (from Oscar Rosenfeld's notebooks): "Police surround houses, take children. Wagons in front of houses. Suddenly screaming women appear, girls, old women, up into the wagon, children thrown on like packages. In front, a *Feldgrau* with whip, soldiers with rifles, revolvers, steel helmets. Window must be shut. Pressing of faces to the window." Here is another by Jozef Zelkowicz: "On Rybna Street the police have to take people out of their apartments. There they are encountering resistance. There they rip babies from their mother's breast, drag grown children from under their parents wings. There they tear husband from wife." Both can be found (with many others) in the compilation *Lodz Ghetto: Inside a Community Under Siege*, compiled and edited by Alan Adelson and Robert Lapides (New York: Viking, 1989). The epigram at the beginning of this book is from a poem also found in this book.

This much I always knew about her past because she had told me when I was very young, but no more: She had been married and she had a son who lived until he was three. Once there was in our possession also a wedding photo, now gone. It was a black and white close-up of my mother as a young bride. She was lovely, wearing a white gown and headdress ("not white, but very light pink," she assured me). Lodz's main street today is full of wedding boutiques. Was it on *ul* Piotrkowska that this gown had been ordered and bought? Or did a favorite seamstress come to her house using precious fabric her family had set aside for this purpose? She ordered most of her clothes from a seamstress who made them for her from style photos and cloth samples. The family traded in fine goods, among them bolts of silk cloth and lace. Throughout my recent researches, I had always to remember that all her records from the war years (and even after) are in the name of Kromolowska, not Sierardzka. Several times I was almost deceived when I found other Bluma Sierardzkas (variously spelled, and several from Zdunska Wola, very likely her cousins) in the records.

Only once while my mother lived did I creep close to the sacred place. Sensing that one day she would no longer be able to answer, I asked and she told me his name and that he was born in June. I wrote down the name and then carried it with me always, but never knew it until now. *Wolf Leib Kromolowski* (wolf and lion). Because I had that name with me in Poland, I found his birth certificate and his father's name in the registry of births (and burials but not of these lost souls) in Lodz. He was born, my half brother, on June 20, 1939. I, too, would bear a son in June and give him two Hebrew names for living things, quite by chance, since he was named after his grandfather, my father Chaim Hersh (life and deer).

My brother, even unnamed, had been part of my fantasy life from the time I was very young and became more so as I moved into my teen years. I must have confused him with my uncle Avrum (who had a name and a picture). As a young teenager I daydreamed that we would find him and that I would, therefore, have a living older brother. This older brother was a romantic fixation—someone to look up to and to introduce me to his friends. My mother had spent years searching for her older brother, and to me the two stories somehow merged. But, of course, my mother knew that my older brother was dead, while hers she always imagined might still be alive somewhere.

Much later in my childhood, after my cousin Bella came to visit us, my mother told me that my father, too, had lost a family. I was probably about seven, and it came as a shock. It was a shock to learn that his family had been so full, so well-formed, so complete. "He had four children," she said. "The oldest son was already grown when they went to Auschwitz." Two boys and two girls—two men and two women—they were when they were wiped out (*vernichtet*), devoured in Auschwitz. She also told me about the picture. (See photo p. 115.) The whole family existed, was portrayed, could be seen, in a photograph that was now in Israel. My Tante Brandel had the photo, and my mother had seen it once in Germany; but my father refused to look at it, or keep it, so it remained with Tante Brandel who took it with her to Israel. "They were a beautiful family," my mother told me. He had married young, and so when the time came when only he survived, he was old, and some of the children were already grownup. How old, I wanted to know. "One," she told me, "was about twenty, another close to that. The other two were younger."

The picture, the ages, the names were all a mystery to me, and would remain so. They were a haunting, not a tragic past like my mother's family. But when I asked my mother about the name of her son, I also asked the names of his children. Only one child did I ever overhear him talk about—the youngest girl (I always imagined that she was the youngest child), clearly his favorite. "She was beautiful and fair-haired," I heard him say, unlike either of her black-haired parents and all her other siblings. And she might have survived if he had been willing to give her up to the ghetto official who wanted to keep her. But he could not "give her away," as he put it, "or choose one over the others." He had tried to hide all the children he said, and the official, likely well paid off, could not continue hiding them. I never really understood.

Only now, after going to Poland, with some shreds of records before me, have I started to piece it together, now that the children have become real and their lives a possibility. She was called Henja, and she was the next youngest child, not the youngest. *Henja Malka Fass* was born in Lodz on January 20, 1933; she was therefore eleven and one-half years old when the Germans liquidated the Lodz ghetto and transported the forty thousand remaining Jews to Auschwitz. (She would have been two years younger if she too was taken in the *Gesperre*.) At Auschwitz they were then processing Jews so quickly (from Poland and Hungary) that they could not keep enough gas in stock and gave up tattooing numbers on the arms of those few selected to work. It is possible that my father and his whole family stayed longer in Lodz even than most of those who had remained until this ending. These others were almost all gone by mid-August. This was the impression he always gave. They were hidden, or the officials well enough paid to overlook them. Eventually, however, they all reported for transportation. ("How long can you hide and not know?" he explained when I asked why he came out of hiding. "We waited for the Allies to come.")[2] Then they all left—he, his wife, my grandmother Sheindel with my father's cousin Chana and the four children (was it four? or two?).

Today, I know all their names. My father had four children with whom he went to Auschwitz. In addition to Henja, they were *Brajna (Brandel)*, the oldest, born December 31, 1929, *Szabsaj David (Shepsel)*, born August 1, 1931, and the youngest child, *Abraham Izaak*, born June 15, 1934. All of them were *Fass*. In 1944 none of these children was more

---

2. My father may have been waiting for the Russians to cross the Vistula River to liberate Warsaw. They had already crossed the Bug River in July 1944 (before the liquidation of the Lodz ghetto) and liberated the eastern part of Poland. But the Russian army sat across the Vistula River until the Warsaw uprising was crushed. The Russians did not enter Warsaw until January 1945.

than fifteen years of age according to their birth certificates, and the youngest was just past ten. It is possible that he lied about their ages to the ghetto authorities so that he didn't have to turn them over when young children were rounded up and he thus remembered them as older. It is possible that he lied when he registered their births in Lodz and that they were, in fact, older than their records state. It is possible even that he deceived himself about how long he was able to keep them alive. I will never know.

I will also never know why the two youngest children, Abraham and Henja, were not registered as living with the rest of the family during the last ghetto census of 1944. They seem to have simply disappeared. When I

The photograph of my father and his first family before the destruction, which he would not look at or keep with him. Portrayed are (from the left) my father's wife Alta Isbicka Fass, his oldest son Szabsaj David (Shepsel), his youngest daughter Henja Malka, his youngest son, Abraham Isaak, my father, and his oldest daughter Brajna (Brandel). The photograph appears to have been taken in the mid 1930s, a few years before the outbreak of the war.

first saw that only two children were still living with my father and his wife and that he therefore likely went to Auschwitz with only two, I thought maybe he had deceived himself about this. In his grief and desire to keep them alive, that he remembered having saved all four children through all those years (until the very end), when it had only been two. But now I think otherwise. In January 1943, my father and his family are described as having relocated in the ghetto from 16 Masarska to 13 Storchen. In fact, these were two names for the same street; the Germans systematically changed Polish street names to German ones. The relocation and technical change in address, however, means that it was perhaps possible to hide people behind those facts. At this point the two youngest children disappear from the records. It was probably then that my father hid them by giving them over to someone else to protect, or with the compliance of a ghetto official (German or Jew?) hid the fact that they were still alive and living with him (or near him). He had told me that he always managed to obtain supplies of food in the ghetto (potatoes he grew himself) to feed his family. He must have bribed people with food in a ghetto where extreme hunger was the major source of mortality and a daily reality for everyone. The ghetto was repeatedly starved by the German authorities and the Jewish overseers, and food was at an enormous premium. My father's "occupation" in the Lodz ghetto was to sort the clothes, bedding, and other goods left behind when the Jews arrived in the ghetto, and then again what remained when they were transported out of the ghetto further along the chain of death. Among their things, he found jewelry, money, and silver, which he was required to turn over to the German officials. He may have managed to keep some of these in order to bribe ghetto officials. One story my father told me pointed toward this conclusion. "One day, an officer knocked on the door at night. 'Harry,' he said, 'give me the jewelry.' There, I replied, over above the sink you can find my wedding ring and my wife's wedding ring. That is all I have. Take them." Behind this story was a hidden story, one that suggested that at times my father had other things to offer, things this officer, or others, expected to receive.

So he hid them, the two youngest ones, until the bitter end.[3] Perhaps, this was the meaning of what I had overheard as a child. He could not chose one child over another when the ghetto official offered to keep only the fairer-haired girl. He had spent his life in the war protecting them all. He hid them from roundups, and he hid them from starvation, and he almost hid them from me. But I know that the written records can and do lie, but that whatever his self-deception concerning their ages, my father would not have lied about this: *He went to Auschwitz with all four children, his wife, his mother, and his cousin, and only he and his cousin Chana survived.*

I always thought that it was strange that my father should have survived but that his "grown" children had been sent in the wrong direction—to the left during the selection at Auschwitz-Birkenau, while he went to the right. My memory may have been confused when my mother described his children as grown; she likely meant that they would now (in the mid-1950s) be quite grown, about the same age as my cousin Bella. But I know now that the children were not grown, though the war experience hardly left them children. Even the oldest was not yet fifteen and the littlest one, stunted by four years in the ghetto no doubt, was just ten. Whether my own confusion or my father's memory of them misled

3.   There are serious discrepancies between the ghetto records that I saw at the Lodz archives center and the Lodz Ghetto registry online at *Jewish Gen*. In the online service Szabsaj David together with his mother Alta Izbicka are listed as transported out of the ghetto on January 22, 1943, and Abram Izak [stet](the youngest of the children), two weeks earlier, on January 8, 1943. The two girls, Brajna and Henja Malka are not recorded as having been deported or transported. In this version of the registry, all family members were first registered on January 20, 1943, when they were moved from Rast Weg to Storchen Gasse 13. In this record my father's wife and his two sons were taken the month they were first registered (very late for Jews from Lodz) in the ghetto, and the youngest child even earlier. Only my father and his daughters remained in the ghetto to the end (together with my grandmother Sheindel and Chana Fass). If this record is correct, then my father was hiding them before 1943 and not later, and, at this point, when his youngest child could no longer be hidden and was deported, he decided that all of them should come out of hiding and be registered. Because these records are problematic and contradictory, this information may simply suggest that those who are recorded as deported were hidden, despite the fact that they were supposed to have been already gone.

me, I now know that those were young children he took with him (or
were taken from him) to the selection point where Dr. Josef Mengele (or
some other demon) determined who was to live and who was to die (and
chose from among the children the subjects of his sadistic science), those
brothers and sisters I never knew and didn't even fantasize about.

The youngest girl I had heard about because she must have been his
favorite (and he had almost saved her from her fate by giving her away).
She was described as blond, but she was hardly that in the photograph
when I finally saw it. My sister's light brown hair and my daughter's
blond must have stabbed his heart and stirred up memories of a child
who had been somewhat fairer haired than the other five members of
his large young family. It was indeed a full family and one of which he
was clearly proud. The photo proclaims this pride everywhere. He never
wanted children after the war, my mother told me (not even girls?).
She, who did very much want them, had persuaded him to acquiesce in
middle age and so we were born, my sister and I, six years apart, my sister
when he was almost fifty. Although, like so much else concerning my
father, I really don't know exactly how old he was then. He remembered
his children as older and possibly remembered himself as older too.

His wife was very dark-haired, pretty, and kind, my Tante Brandel
said. He was lucky, she insisted, twice to marry good-natured women
who indulged him and let him have his way. Now I know her name and
her birth date. *Alta Izbicka Fass* was born on March 3, 1904. Though Alta
means old, she looks like a sweet young girl in the photograph. Izbicka
sounds strange and foreign even in a country full of strange-sounding
names. It was probably Polish, but it might have been from some more
distant place. Could it be Bosnian? The news today is filled with names
like these. Nawry, my grandmother Pola's maiden name, is also odd and
unusual even in Poland. I have read that it was based on the town of
Navre, in West Prussia (Thorn of Prussia). Poland, which didn't exist
through most of the nineteenth century, was a gathering place for Jews
from all over central Europe, from the German west, the Russian east,

Austria, and possibly even as far south as the Balkans. And they brought their names with them. They met and married from among Jews who had spent time among many nations. Some brought *yiches* and some did not. And they all died together in Chelmno and Auschwitz, Treblinka and Belzec, Sobibor and Bergen Belsen, Warsaw and Lodz and hundreds of other places, large and small. They died as old people and young children, dark-haired and fair. Male and female created He them, and male and female they were led into the gas chamber. Two and two, two boys and two girls into the ovens.

CHAPTER 6

MY PARENTS

My parents' very different pasts came together in Auschwitz. Different in character, in class, in outlook on life, all of this fell away as the Lodz Ghetto dissolved, and each confronted the aloneness of the camps, the aloneness of surviving, and the solitary need to reflect on what surviving would mean. One reads about survivor's guilt, and, no doubt, both my parents suffered profoundly in this manner. My father never forgave himself for outliving his children, for failing to save them from doom. But the fact of surviving led also to other emotions in both of my parents, emotions ranging from vindication against the Nazis to gratitude for the possibilities still available to them. My mother expressed this through an intense desire to bear children. She was grateful for the opportunity to make life happen again. She also had a keen sense of responsibility expressed through both her Judaism as a form of continuity with the past and her commitment to telling her story.

My father's sense of aloneness was always more intense than my mother's, but even he could occasionally look forward to frame a possible life, and as a proud man he took some pleasure in the sheer fact of being alive, although taking pleasure is not an experience I connect easily with my father. Still, as I look back as an adult, I admit to being baffled by their urge to continue living, by their willingness to wrench from their pain and loss the idea of starting again. Maybe my father was right to turn his back on the portrait of his family. How else could he save any space to breathe? Maybe survival required an altogether unthinking commitment to self-preservation, a commitment that carried them through the camps and then carried them through a new life. When my father spoke of his time in the camps, he usually emphasized endurance over anything else. My father could endure hunger, cold, and hard work. He made himself endure the losses as well.

It is not clear to me how my parents met, how they emerged from the death watch of the camps to make claims on a pretended normality after their separate liberations—my mother's from Bergen-Belsen where she went after Auschwitz, my father's from Ahlem, one of the several labor camps to which he was sent. By the time I picked up the story, they were in Hannover, Germany, in the British zone of occupation, a gathering place for survivors, where they married on June 25, 1946. (Their wedding was celebrated at a party on July 14, 1946; see photograph and party invitation.) They had met through friends, was all I was ever told. And I have photos of them with various friends taken shortly after the end of the war. I was born eleven months later in the same city, on the Ohestrasse, next to a rose garden. I have a ridiculously clear memory of this place, with its steep front steps and common hall toilet, with the smell of roses everywhere.

We lived with others like ourselves, with friends who would last through my childhood, our transition to America, through summers in the Catskills, and into my wedding. We were a band of survivors and their children. Everyone who could had a child as quickly as possible in Germany; eventually they all had at least two.[1] This included my parents, although they were among the oldest of their group of friends.

---

1.   This common pattern is confirmed by Atina Grossmann in an essay on the life of Jews in Germany after their liberation. The essay appears in *Life After Death: Approaches to a Cultural and Social History of Europe during the 1940s and 1950s,* edited by Richard Bessel and Dirk Schumann (Cambridge: Cambridge University Press, 2003).

One of several photographs taken at my parents' wedding reception in July 1946, with an invitation to the event.

None of their friends had lost so many children in that earlier life. I know this now in ways that I did not realize at the time, although several times I did ask my mother which of her friends had children before the war. Most, she told me, had been younger and still unmarried, but a few had been married. Tante Edja had also lost a child ("I think he was also a boy," my mother said when I asked her one summer in the country). My parents had already had one life and now set upon having another. No one spoke then about post-traumatic stress or the psychological costs of their many losses. No one gave them advice or counsel. Instead, they set out on their own to create a new future for themselves and their new children. I thought of them as heroes, people with great strength and fortitude, people I hugely admired, despite their many disadvantages.

———

My mother and father had been born before Poland was recreated out of the European collapse of World War I, and both had suffered the profound deprivations that war had brought to its Eastern front. In the early 1920s my father was a teenager when the Poles finally fought off the newly formed Soviet Union to achieve the independence Polish patriots had sought for more than a hundred years. My mother was a young girl, but she remembered and recounted the constant hunger she experienced when a family of five had to share the heel of one loaf of bread for supper. She who loved dolls had to make one from an old rag because real ones were far too dear. She sometimes missed going to school because she had no shoes to wear, and her father was actually taken to prison for this delinquency. On the other side of Lodz in Balut, where my father lived exclusively among Jews, such delinquencies apparently went unnoticed because few children in his family (at least not among the older ones) attended secular school. The boys, including my father, went to *heder*, the common Yiddish school of European Jewry, which had been in place for hundreds of years before the *Haskalah* (Jewish Enlightenment) that was supposed to liberate Jews into civil society. Whatever the obvious disadvantages accompanying such a ghettoized existence, it seemed mercifully free of the officialdom that plagued the aspirations of those who lived more fully among Poles. Apparently, these children were never forced to attend a secular Polish school.

Poverty somewhere in the past was common to most of the survivors we knew, though few talked openly about it. A very few came from genuinely privileged families where they had been pampered and indulged; others fantasized a privileged past life they never lived. My mother often observed that without witnesses left to their past—no neighbors or family or friends—many transformed themselves. Some claimed to come from the city nearest the *shtetl* in which they had been born; some proclaimed their birth to the families of wealth or distinction that they may have observed around them. In this way, thanks to the war's destructiveness, America offered people not just upward economic mobility in the future but also social mobility in the past. Very few admitted that those who were most likely to survive the ghetto and the camps (insofar as anything other than blind dumb luck made any difference) were those who had learned early how to endure the cruel deprivations of food, warmth, and hope that the Nazis imposed on all Jews, regardless of origins—those from small towns and large cities, both working class and middle class, the illiterate and the intelligentsia.

My parents had both known extreme want in their childhoods because they lived through a war whose equal none hoped to witness again. By the time that terrible first war was over, my father was already in business for himself—a dealer in used merchandise. With his partner Hainoch, he traveled among the small towns and big cities of the new Polish nation gathering goods and making money. My father always told stories about those "good" times when he and Hainoch stopped at inns and restaurants for meals and prowled freely in the Jewish quarters of Poland, from Lodz to Lublin. The story I treasure concerned the eating habits of the two partners: My father, always provident, ate his potatoes first and saved for last the much-anticipated portion of meat, while his partner immediately ate his meat, just "in case the bombs should fall" to interrupt their repast. Each had developed a different strategy to deal with the adversity he knew would find them sooner or later. Hainoch, my father once told me, was taken in one of the earliest selections from the Lodz ghetto, although it is doubtful that he had enjoyed a portion of meat before his deportation.

By trading and traveling, my father had also learned the ways of the world, and he had begun the life of constant toil that made him a good provider all his life. First, he had supported his parents, brothers, and sisters while he was still in his teens during World War I and afterward when life in Poland returned to "normal." Soon he married and settled down to the life of a fairly prosperous, hard-working family man. The children came every couple of years, starting in the late 1920s. That first child, Brandel (Brajna) was born on December 31, 1929, if we are to believe her birth certificate. (That date, the last possible day of the 1920s, makes it possible, though unlikely, that someone may have tried to squeeze the recording of the event into this final slot.) These must have been the good times of my father's life, as he took pride in his growing and attractive family, in his ability to earn a living, and the respect he gained in the community for all of those things—for being a good son, a good father, a good *ferdiner* (provider). He was also independent, something he sought once again when we came to the United States. He wanted no overseers or bosses. He could work himself harder than anyone else. By the early 1930s, he must have laughed at his good fortune in that wonderful way that I remember so well, in which he seemed to forget his surroundings and inhibitions and greet God face-to-face. I always associated this laugh with the telling Yiddish line in Dzigan and Szumacher (a Yiddish comic team). "Me ken leben, no man lost nisht." (Loosely translated, "life could be great but it's not allowed.") Black haired and very handsome, with beautiful facial structure and a dimpled chin, he might have imagined that he left adversity behind by the early 1930s when (according to the birth certificate) his fourth child Abraham Isaak was born on June 1934.

In 1934, my mother was still unmarried at twenty-four, no longer very young. She lived a full life, earning a living by trading luxury goods in the family business. She had friends among Jews and gentiles, some of them very wealthy, though her family, even in the best of times, lived modestly. Still, there was money for dressmakers who copied the latest Paris styles, for her personal, engraved Jewish New Year's cards printed in Polish (I still have part of one of these), and for visits to the *zukernias* (sweet shops), for coffee or tea in the late afternoon. She came to know one Polish actress quite well (even then Lodz's citizens, crazy about movies, filled many movie theatres as spectators, and international stars stayed at the Hotel Grand and lived in the city). My mother brought expensive goods to the actress on approval—yards of silk brocades for dresses and drapes as well as Persian rugs, Czechoslovakian crystal, and other *objets d'art*. Trusting my mother's taste, this woman allowed my mother to find and bring goods for her and then selected what she wanted (much in the manner of interior decorators today but much more extensively to include personal items). This woman, my mother told me, was the mistress of a German industrialist who came to visit her regularly on his frequent trips to Lodz. At these times, my mother was hurried from the apartment through a back way. Her most vivid and brutal memory of this relationship concerned the time the lover insisted on mating his very large German shepherd with the small poodle the actress adored. The little dog died as a result.

There were lots of Germans in Lodz even before the war. Some of the largest and most prosperous industrial concerns, such as Geyer, were run by Germans in a city that came into existence in the mid-nineteenth century as an outpost of the industrializing West. There was a large and conspicuous Protestant ("evangelical") church on the main street, and my mother spoke German even before the Nazis occupied the city.

I am not sure how my mother was able to reconcile her own Jewish orthodoxy with either an acquaintance with this kind of woman friend or her friendship with other Poles. She seemed to cherish the memory of this woman and the others. The gradual modernization of Jewish Poland between the wars must have taken place in just this way, through a more-or-less comfortable extension outward of the younger members of the Orthodox Jewish community into the secular world around them. My mother wore fashionable clothes, had her hair bobbed short and marceled (hand waved), spoke Polish, and worked before she married. She went to the movies and ate outside the house (although probably only sweets and pastries). She listened to modern music and read modern literature. She hung out with people her age. She had grown up in the 1920s and into young womanhood in the early 1930s. Although her life was not exactly like that of the American young people I had studied in my first book on the American 1920s, neither was it so very different. Young orthodoxy in Poland, while clinging to Jewish life, moved inexorably into the twentieth century. Still there were very clear limits. My mother once told me: "One day, I received a huge bouquet of flowers with a card from a young male admirer." Because he was not Jewish, her mother forced her "to send it back. This was painful to me and humiliating." My

A photograph of my mother, Bluma Sieradzka, seated on the left (with a friend standing to her right) taken when she was in her late teens in Poland in the late 1920s.

uncle Jerry, younger than my mother, had probably moved even further from the circle of tradition than my mother: hatless, beardless, carefree, and modern with a silver cigarette case (for others) in his pocket.

She must have been reluctant to marry because she knew how much she would give up, though she was never rebellious enough to reject entirely the Orthodox match that was certain to be her portion and the traditional life that would follow. (She told me that she had refused several offers.) Finally, however, she did marry, the son of a very distinguished Hasidic family, known for their learning, piety, and good works. I would guess that he himself was probably not distinguished because by then she was well into her twenties; her reluctance had probably cost her more affluent choices. I simply don't know. Perhaps it was a love match like that of her parents. He may also have been a great scholar. Her parents were relieved, no doubt, and even she, by then, must have been intrigued by the possibilities that came with marriage, especially the birth and rearing of children which she very much desired. She could hardly have been intrigued by what she knew were the burdens of running an observant Jewish household, having borne so much of it already in her father's house.

She never talked about him, Zajnwel Kopel Kromolowski,[2] or about their marriage, which took place in 1938. Soon thereafter she lived once more with her parents, this time in that Jewish ghetto they had avoided all their lives. This short piece of independent married life could hardly have made much of an impression; it passed so quickly into another world.

––––––

"I was sitting in the park on the afternoon of September 1, 1939, with my mother and the baby in a carriage, when my father came to tell us that the war had begun." When she was very sick and I knew she was dying, I began to ask her for a more systematic recounting of her experiences.

2.   My mother spelled her married name, Krimalowski (as on her wedding party invitation), but I have adopted the spelling from her son's birth certificate.

This is as far as we got. It was obviously too late to probe for the past when there was nothing but past left to her. But I will always remember her first experience of the devastation that was soon to follow the outbreak of World War II in her words, words that so well captured place and time and the people she was soon to lose. It punctured my heart when in May 2000 I saw this park in Poland, the park that lay between the Lodz she had grown up in and the poorer, more parochial, outlying district of Lodz she was about to discover. She lived on the other side for four years, first all of them together and then only with her mother, my grandmother Pola, after her father and husband had died and the child had been torn away. By the end the household had also merged with that of her brother, Avrum.

My father knew the ghetto very well. Since childhood, he had explored its possibilities, and he put that to good use during the four years he spent there not as an independent businessman, but under the Nazi lash. He sorted clothes and bedding and other possessions brought into the ghetto by the tens of thousands (by the end, hundreds of thousands) of Jews—first from the rest of Lodz, then from the smaller towns in the surrounding area and other Polish cities, and finally from countries in the West. Lodz became a transportation depot in the chain of Jewish destruction, a stopover for Jews destined for Chelmno, Auschwitz, and Treblinka. Lodz was a place for the in-gathering of Central and Western European Jews, especially after many other ghettos were destroyed or closed. My father, very good at his work, became a supervisor of the *sortierei* set up as Lodz was turned into a workshop for the war. Here goods that could either be used by German soldiers and civilians or transformed into war materièl were separated by type into huge lofts of goods and sent to places throughout the expanding Reich and its many fronts. My father was an excellent worker and stayed alive because he was useful. He was also asked to turn over to the corrupt local officials any valuables he found stashed among the goods, jewelry or money somehow hidden after repeated demands to turn them over to either the Nazis or the local Jewish council had reduced the inhabitants to the last ditches of evasion as they sought to salvage some remnant of their former selves or as a means to bribe their way to extra food. Chaim Rumkowski, the Jewish doctor who became "King" of the Lodz Ghetto, had required that everyone turn over their valuables and their labor in the effort to demonstrate what good and profitable Reich workers Jews could be. In this way, Rumkowski probably saved my father's life and for a time that of his family, though my father did not know Rumkowski personally and hated him thoroughly. In return, Rumkowski starved the ghetto inhabitants through an extremely tight rationing system, which literally measured an ever stingier allocation of calories per day.

My father, the provider, always had some food for his family because he had a small plot somewhere in the dank ghetto where he grew potatoes (or knew how to acquire them from the outside) and he knew where to hide his children when others were rounded up. He also knew how to bribe officials with the trinkets he found and with the furs that the wealthy, modern Jews from the West were forced to leave behind as they boarded the cattle cars to the carefully hidden places of extermination that had been assigned to them when the Wandsee Conference launched its plan for the "final solution" to Europe's nagging Jewish problem. That "problem" had included Jewish overreaching in the achievement of excess wealth and underachievement in widespread Jewish poverty; too many Jewish doctors and lawyers in Budapest and too many Jewish manufacturers in Lodz, too many Jewish communists in Warsaw, too many Jewish rabbis in Vilna, and too many Jewish rabble-rousers in the streets of Berlin. In the end, all the Jewish troublemakers could be neatly dealt with by bringing them together in Poland, which became the charnel house of Europe. For all the Jews who came through Lodz on their journeys to the German solution, my father sorted their clothes and other belongings.

The Lodz ghetto was a hellhole in which my parents spent four years of their adult lives. Shut off from the Christian part of the city, occupied by Germans, (except for two and then one carefully controlled overpass bridge), it became a workshop producing clothes, rag rugs and straw mats (on which my mother worked), shoes (her husband worked on these), and other products out of the muscle, sinew, and finally the vital organs of its imprisoned Jewish population. It was run by its *Judenrat*, just as other ghettoed places were, but in fact it was the brain child of Chaim Rumkowski, whose bargain with the Nazi devil was to keep as many Jews as possible alive in exchange for the labor power that made them indispensable to the Reich. He saw it as a point of honor to put all the inhabitants of Lodz to useful occupations (including both the young and the old as long as they lasted). He might have invented another saying to precede the Auschwitz gate, *"Arbeit Oder Tot"* (work or death). As a result, the Jews of Lodz earned their right to continue living, or at least some of them could continue living as others starved and died of the diseases of the ghetto—typhus, dysentery and tuberculosis—or were sent off to their deaths in the repeated selections that even Rumkowski's promises of labor could not stave off. In the end some of them managed to fend off death. Those who survived the starvation rations and the accelerating selections to death camps like Chelmno, earned the right to make it to Auschwitz. To this final symbol of the freedom offered by work the last remaining inhabitants of this last Jewish ghetto of Europe were driven when the ghetto was officially closed in August 1944, as the Soviet army slowly began its move toward the city.

The Lodz ghetto was without escape, without sewers, without resources of exchange with the outside (they used their own currency with Rumkowki's face on it), but it was a ghetto that Rumkowski strung along on the hope of more time. In this he succeeded. Its inhabitants were starved and worked nearly to death, but the Lodz ghetto contributed the largest number of survivors out of Poland to the postwar world. They survived not only because the Lodz inhabitants reached Auschwitz late but also because the conditions at Auschwitz were but one step beyond Lodz. That step was the selection that left isolated individuals still alive moving in one direction toward life after their kin went to their deaths in the other. There were no parting goodbyes outside the invisible Birkenau gate, where my mother saw her mother and her niece for the last time as they were directed to the showers. Though my uncle Avrum survived the selection in his male-only line, he still did not survive the war. My mother clung to the knowledge that he had made it past the selection, but past the selection was also a world of death.

My father was also on the men's only line. His mother, his wife, and his two daughters had disappeared in the crowd of women. But in that line he stood with his sons whom he was sure would survive. After all they were young and as strong as four years of the Lodz ghetto and my father's carefully cultivated plot and endless labor could make them. But in the end, they wound up where he was sure it was his fate to go and he never could forget that final parting with his two "grown sons."[3] (Their birth certificates put them at ten and fourteen years of age). He always thought it had to have been his fault—his failure of guidance or protection or just his stinking good luck to look younger than his years. My father was a survivor and proud of his survival skills, but this particular instance he could neither forgive nor forget. The pain of saving them for four years through hell and then losing them finally in an *augenblick* (blink of an eye) was too much even for his well-burdened life to bear. I always knew when he was thinking of them, sitting there quietly in his chair with his head in his hands. Later, when he was an old man, he used to pace up and down the corridor in our house, his hands behind his back. His pacing became a way of warding off the demons. It was probably a good thing that we, his second family, were all women—two daughters and a granddaughter (the only grandchild he ever knew). My father had parted with daughters, too, but at that very last moment of a past life, he must have reached out to but could not save his sons.

3.   As noted in chapter 5, some ghetto records indicate that his younger son had been deported almost two years before this time.

After they were parted from everyone they had loved, each of my parents then had a bowl for soup and a worn, rough blanket to cover him/herself on the narrow shelf to which they were assigned. Each was alone. Their heads shaven, women as well as men, their clothes useless against the elements, treated like animals—they were humiliated whenever possible. They were the driven of the earth. In the very early morning, still very dark and very cold, they were driven out for *Appell*, for work details, or for selection, or to dig ditches, or just for the sake of the official's satisfaction in demonstrating sheer power over them. They guarded their bread rations and their bowls, sometimes sleeping with remnants of their allotted portions of bread as a pillow under their heads. They guarded their shoes. My mother had only wooden clogs at Bergen-Belsen. But all this is well known. In the camps, their lives were the numbers they were given. Only their memories were their own, and the skills to survive on less and less food and more and more cold, as September became December and January and then February, in Poland and then in Germany where many were sent after Auschwitz to other *lagers* (work camps).

My father, surprisingly, had stories of occasional kindness in *katzet* (concentration camp). The Belgian doctor for whom he worked in the infirmary saved him several times from both the excruciating work roundups that would probably have killed him in the deep pits of Ahlem and the certain death that came from selections. (Primo Levi also gives an account of such a doctor in *Survival in Auschwitz*.) This Catholic, political prisoner saw and cherished my father as a son, but eventually he himself was among the victims of the selection. My father also described the times he was asked to place an extra portion of soup beneath the infirmary bunk that my uncle Abram Sieradzki sometimes occupied because he was considered, even in that place, a decent and worthy man. Even a German officer who saw my father steal some vegetable peelings from the large heap outside the officer's mess (absolutely off limits to inmates), excoriated him and chased him away, but he did not whip or kill him as he might have done, a kindness in itself. My mother's one story of kindness was more limited. Ordered to sweep a floor, she was merely reprimanded rather than whipped or beaten when she had not done it as meticulously as the overseer had demanded. More oddly, she told me that she had indeed not done a very good job (even in hell, my mother set standards for herself). Survival came from such tiny gestures and from sheer brutal luck. My father, together with many of the male Lodz survivors of the Auschwitz selection, was sent to a series of labor camps, Ahlem among them, between 1944 and 1945, as Jews were forced to work for German firms such as Maschenfabrik Niedersachsen, Hannover, a producer of tanks and other munitions that were meant to hold off the Allies. They worked to keep themselves enslaved, while they heard the Allied bombardment near by. Many of them, but not my father, dug deep underground tunnels to hide the armaments they made.

My mother went through Auschwitz, where she stayed for just a few weeks, on her way to Bergen-Belsen. But she stayed long enough to watch the Jewish women of Greece disappear overnight into the ashes. According to my mother, one day they were there in the camp, and the next they were gone. The Jewish community of Salonika had thrived for six hundred years, a sanctuary from the Spanish expulsion with its origins stretching back to pre-Christian days and a major center of Jewish learning and culture during the height of the Ottoman period. They were beautiful girls, she recalled, fiery-eyed and full of life.

In Bergen-Belsen, my mother survived as a forced laborer who worked on munitions. She and those with whom she shared her hut and her work learned to negotiate with each other and with their German overseers. Here she became a kind of spokeswoman, not shy and not afraid (what else could she lose?). And here she saw others steal from each other. The women were bald and constantly hungry and always cold. They stole each other's bowls, and they stole each other's bread, and they stole each other's right to survive. They shared filthy latrines. A few survived even this, and they came to America to wear furs and diamonds and bleach their hair blond. She once told me that she saw someone she later called a friend steal another's blanket. She remembered it always, and it always bothered her, but she rejoiced when this woman—blond and prosperous—married and bore two sons and lived well in later life.

Survival, neither an art nor a moral act, was a fact that came to some out of the infinite minutiae of the calculus of daily unpredictability. My mother was liberated by the English, who, she claimed, never let down their icy reserve even in the presence of once beautiful girls and women turned into ugly scarecrows. "The English soldiers did not cry," she said. But the books I have read describe the British as "in shock" by what they found in Bergen-Belsen.

My mother and several of her close friends from Bergen-Belsen— Regina, Basia, Chava, and Sabina—went together to Hannover, which was a gathering point for the displaced. And there they met others, women and men, Bella and Shulim, Edja and Natan, Bronka and Jacob and made a life. And they bore children, if they still could. They started new lives in the birthplace of the classical German language, amidst the rubble of streets, near the spectacular and war-spared gardens of the ancestors of the current English royal house, Herrenhausen. I do not remember the beautiful grounds of Herrenhausen, but we have photos of this place that we visited often, usually with other *tantes* and their children. In some of these I am happily feeding the birds who literally eat out of my hand; in others I am standing on top of a statue. Instead, I remember the fragrant rose garden immediately next to our house, so full of colors and the gardener's huge shears. I also recall the apartment we lived in, with a tiny kitchen and a very large front room dominated by its fireplace and my parents' bed. And I remember walking on the rubble which littered the streets. Even in Hannover, after the war, the unpredictable continued to haunt my parents' lives. My mother was nearly killed when she stood on a chair to change a light bulb and a soldier's stray bullet whizzed past her head. And here, despite the beautiful big wheeled pram in which I lay, my mother found a rat standing on my face.

Here, amidst the afterward of war, life began again. The survivors were supported mostly by charitable institutions that distributed international relief, like the Joint Distribution Committee (known as the Joint) as well as by supplies provided by the Allied soldiers who were now positioned in Germany, according to their allocated zones. My father also had occasional jobs, like the time he served as MP when Mayor Fiorello LaGuardia came to visit the city. (I remember a photograph of him with his special armband and tall boots.) My father was also one of the very first to receive reparations payments (*Rente*) from the German government; his was a test case that began a notable attempt by the German government to make some retribution to the few Jews who remained after the European slaughter. Thus even in this temporary station, on the way to Palestine or New York or sometimes Toronto, many began to earn, sometimes through black market trade in scarce goods, such as cigarettes and coffee, in an economy unhinged from all moorings. As a result, they also began to spend and to acquire. Germans now looked to the Jews who had access to Allied soldiers and Jewish agencies for resources to put their own lives together. It was easy to find German girls to help care for the children who began to arrive, and drivers for cars. My mother found excellent dressmakers who hand-sewed suits and blouses for her and dresses and coats for me. And there were plenty of pretty things in Germany still—the precious debris of war—silver, porcelain and crystal, watches and jewelry, even jade and cloisonné. And my mother, with her eye for the luxury items she had once sold to others, knew what was worth a second look.

My mother and her friends brought barrels of things to America. My uncle was an exception. He either arrived too late from Poland or left too early for the United States or had no taste for the business of acquisition. We had down comforters wrapped in satin ticking which made our American neighbors (used to harsh wool blankets) laugh at such old-fashioned things, beautiful hand-embroidered linens with monograms for the table and the bed, old Rosenthal china, hand-wrought silver, and Leica cameras. I had bags of toys, including classic Steiff dolls. We came

My father, Chaim Harry Fass, in Hannover, Germany, after the war. The photograph is probably taken around 1950 just before we came to the United States.

to America with barrels of goods—the wretched refuse of Europe's wars. We, whose lives and property had been stolen by Germans and Ukrainians, Poles and Slovaks, Hungarians and Frenchmen, brought the goods of all these nations to America. We also brought the accumulated lessons of survival—obey the laws, learn the language, save your money, and guard your children.

———

Our trip across the Atlantic, in frigid January, on an army munitions boat, the *Admiral Muir,* was an ordeal of high seas and storms, sickness and separation. I was in and out of the ship's infirmary with a recurrent sore throat (strep?) that was misdiagnosed as "internal" measles. My father lay in his bunk, green from seasickness. Only my mother walked around and worked (required as part of the payment for our passage), sweeping the decks, and she ministered to us both.

The memory of that trip has remained like a glass splinter buried in my brain, an un-dissolved shard of difficult new beginnings. In our female-only dormitory, where I lay on an upper bunk (from which I twice fell), I remember that a woman tried to kill herself one night in the brightly lit, all white communal bathroom. She used a piece of glass to cut her wrists, and the red blood spilled all over the white brightly lit sink. I don't know what happened to her. I went to the hospital soon after that with my high fever and painful throat. When she could, my mother took me to the ship's library where she pretended to read from the English language children's books, making up the words in German as we looked at the illustrations. I especially remember the "Three Little Pigs," which I favored and she read again and again, until it fell apart. In Germany, my mother had taught me the inevitable German children's song, "Hanschen Klein Ging Alein" (Little Hans goes out alone), and we sang it often. Thus, through the whole voyage, its refrain "Aber Mamma weinet sehr" (but mother cries a lot) because her son is no longer around, rang in my ears. It was only much later that I fully understood the importance of this song about a son who goes away and the mother who longs for him.

In the hospital I lay alone wrapped tightly in a blanket waiting for my mother to return and refusing to eat. It was forbidden for her to come because, once I was diagnosed with measles, I was put in quarantine to prevent the spread of the disease throughout the ship. There had been a few cases already. My mother, who had seen plenty of measles, scoffed at this idea, but when she pointed out that I had no spots she was told that I had "internal measles." She thought this was simply nonsense. (She was right, of course, because I had measles later in my childhood.) When she came (she always came), she hid behind the door during the nurse's rounds. Once the doctor found her and threw her out. "If you return again," he threatened, and I overheard, "we will keep her on Ellis Island [by then reserved only for the quarantined] when we arrive in New York." She returned as soon as she could. She brought me fragrant red delicious apples, all I would eat, and I listened in fear and longing through all the sounds of the night, waiting for her. I was very thin by the time we arrived in the United States, having spent ten days at sea. On the last day aboard, she came for me, and she held me up high so that I could see the Statue of Liberty. We were together at last. When he saw us together on the deck, the doctor who had separated us told my mother, "Ihnes kind haben sie, yah" (You have your child, I see). I would have spit in his face. My mother smiled.

I was still sick and had a fever when we moved into the Arlington Hotel in lower Manhattan. And although we were invited to eat for free further uptown in the communal kitchen provided by the Hebrew Immigrant Aid Society (HIAS), my mother bought a single burner and cooked for me in our room. We were refugees, paid for by one Jewish charity or another and the new United Nations refugee relief (UNRRA). This was a position my father found insulting and unbearable. He looked for work immediately. Not knowing anything about New York, he walked all the way to Harlem for his first job interview, a job he was offered but refused to take because it required that he work on Saturday. My father, who was never an especially pious Jew, said he would not work on weekends. He soon found work in Brooklyn (to which he also walked at first) at $50 a week, with weekends off, and we searched for a permanent place to live.

Before we left the Arlington, while my parents were on some errand, I slashed my wrist with my father's razor blade left out on the sink. I remember their extreme alarm when they returned. I wanted to know what it felt like, I suppose, or wanted to cause a commotion, remembering no doubt that earlier blood trickle down into the sink on board the *Admiral Muir*. A female physician came to fix me up; she was the first, and for a long time the only, woman doctor who treated me. She wore a green hat with a small feather on the side and carried a leather satchel.

The apartments we were shown on the lower East Side of Manhattan, the immigrant's traditional home, were not only decrepit, but one of them had a tub in the middle of the kitchen and offered nothing but common toilet facilities. My mother fled in horror from such a possibility. In the end, we settled for a brownstone building at 654 Lafayette

Avenue in the Bedford-Styvesant part of Brooklyn that still flourished as the home of a solid middle-class black community and a declining population of Jews. The Grossmans, our landlords, an elderly orthodox Jewish couple, had middle-class children on the move to better parts of the city and its growing suburbs. One of their children had first lived in the apartment below us when we moved in. After they left a family of orthodox Hungarian refugees, greenhorns just like us, moved in. My mother was by then more experienced and Americanized and helped them out with their own adjustments. The first time I ever watched television was with the Grossmans in their living room where they invited me to join them to see John Cameron Swazey read the news. In return, they sometimes asked me to extinguish the electric lights on the Sabbath. I thus became their *Shabbos goy*, something my parents subsequently prohibited me from doing.

We lived on the top floor, where the limited supply of heat offered by the Grossmans never seemed to reach, and the windowsills were seriously separated from the walls. (I used to throw shiny silver quarters and dimes down the hole as I looked out the shaky windows from my parents' bedroom to the street below.) We ate on an oil cloth-covered table in the little kitchen (white linen on Friday nights and holidays). The shaky cabinet hanging from the top of this kitchen once fell on my mother with all her dishes in it. In this kitchen my mother cooked traditional meals—chicken soup with *rinzfleish* (beef for stronger flavor), stuffed cabbage, carrot stew, real gefilte fish (in the skin), and *choulent* with *kishka* (a bean, potato, and fat stew, like cassoulet) cooked on Friday night for Saturday (left overnight on a very low flame that did not need to be tended)—as we gradually learned to become more American. My sister was born in our third year there. Her crib was in my parents' bedroom. I slept in a tiny room attached to this room. My bedroom space didn't even have a radiator, but it did contain the one closet in the entire apartment. Everything we wore was stored here or in our dressers. The barrels in which our goods came to America, some still packed, were settled permanently on the landing just outside our apartment, and these were the first things visible when you came up the stairs.

My father began the routine he continued throughout his working life, even after he had established a successful business of his own with his partner Bernard Wietschner. He awoke at four o'clock in the morning, dressed, ate a small breakfast, and then left the house before five to take the subway to work. By six o'clock he was at work, where he stood all day sorting clothes and other textiles by quality, fabric, and reusability. After this, the goods were either shredded and reprocessed into reusable wool, cotton, rayon or nylon, or shipped off in enormous packets (bales) to places in Africa, where they were recycled. For years, I assumed that when my father told people he was in "rex," this meant something esoteric, until I realized that he was saying "rags" and that his work was the last stage of what New Yorkers call the rag trade (clothing industry). He returned home at five-thirty in the afternoon, ate dinner, and read his newspaper. His routine was sacred, and we learned to respect it. In our house, we had the *Jewish Daily Forward* (then only in Yiddish) every single day of my childhood, which both my parents read completely and then, much later, also the *New York Times*. (We never read a newspaper with a comic strip in it, and when I was very young "Current Events" time at school was torture for me as I always brought pictures from the *Forward*, whose provenance I tried to hide by pasting over the back.) By eight o'clock my father was in bed to get ready for the next early morning. We had to be very quiet once my father retired in the evenings. Only our weekends were in any way relaxed.

In the evenings my mother helped me with my schoolwork, to the extent that she could, as we sat at the kitchen table. Spelling was easy, math harder because she used different calculating techniques (especially in division), but some things, like social studies, were simply not within her ken. Even before I went to school, she and I had registered at the local public library, located just a block away in the middle of Tompkins Park. I can still visualize this small stone neoclassical building with its three front steps in my mind's eye. Sometimes we went several times a week. At first, she read to me, and then soon I read to myself. I must have taken out every book in the children's collection at least once. Our library cards, hers and mine, were our proudest American possessions. The English dictionary my uncle brought me as my first American birthday present was supplemented by my mother with a Polish-English dictionary that she guarded carefully, making sure not to curl its very thin paper edges. (I still possess this book, but its grey worn binding seems to collapse, empty of meaning without her voice.) My mother helped translate words for me—from English in the book to Polish from the dictionary, then from Polish to German or Yiddish orally to me. Through this mélange of languages, she and I learned some English. My mother also taught me to write my name. This resulted in a reprimand from school in a note to my mother by my American teacher. My mother, she said, should not attempt to instruct me at home. I would have to learn block letter writing before I learned cursive. That same teacher told me that my name was spelled Paula not Pola. My initiation into American schools began in September 1951 when I started kindergarten at P.S. 54 in Brooklyn. This limited one-half day program was not at all easy to get into, and others were ahead of me on the waiting list. But with the help of our well-educated and kind African-American neighbor, Mrs. John O. Killens (her husband was the important author of *Young Blood Hawke*), who served as German-English translator, my mother insisted that my need for this program was great, and I was selected from among many applicants who had been longer on the waiting list. I was a little over four years old.

My parents surrounded me with language, although I had all the disadvantages of both an immigrant childhood and a father who had attended secular school only briefly. But my father's spoken Yiddish was rich and robust, and he read not only the Yiddish press but also the great works of Yiddish literature, and even English classics, such as Shakespeare and Dickens, in Yiddish translations. (He, too, had a library card and he exhausted the small collection of Yiddish books in all the libraries near our various homes.) My mother could speak, read, and write Polish, Yiddish, and German, and she began to work on her English shortly after we arrived. The hybrid spellings and pronunciations of this (to her) strange language were often a source of frustration. As I grew up, I heard their stories of youth, war, loss, and survival (and that of their friends) in the many languages they spoke and I understood. (My father also knew a considerable amount of Hebrew, which he always inflected in the Yiddish manner, but Hebrew was reserved for prayer. It was not a conversational language.) And we went to the Yiddish theatre, still alive in two venues when I was little, where we often saw the diminutive Molly Picon in a variety of roles. Because my parents would not leave me alone and would not have dreamed of engaging a baby sitter, I usually went with them to the last bastion of an older ethnic culture with its various vaudeville acts. But we also went to serious theater productions, such as the *Dybbuk* and the *Jazz Singer*. My parents were especially eager to attend when they learned that someone famous was coming (often someone they had seen in Poland) and we usually attended together with our various survivor friends. These late nights were something I looked forward to as my father ended the evening by carrying me asleep on his back up the three flights of stairs to our apartment where the German barrels filled with our goods greeted us on the landing.

In the end, their stories and these experiences with language became my childhood. But their culture was also a source of shame to me. I always could explain to teachers about my parents' past and thus their foreignness, but friends were another matter. They would not understand. I was uneasy when my parents spoke to me in front of my friends or on the street. Worst of all were the school forms that required me to state my parents' ages (far older than the parents of school friends) and "the highest level of education attained." How could I explain on a form where answers were simply checked off that neither of my parents had technically finished high school and that my father never even finished "elementary school" because he had worked all his life—first to support his parents, then to keep his children alive, and finally to make sure that my sister and I graduated from college. And how could I make others understand that these people were knowledgeable about world affairs, capable of adapting to new and trying circumstances, and literate? Their lives were just too incongruous with the templates that guided American surveys and American educational reckonings. At times, I, who wanted to be an American, held my parents responsible for the incongruity, but at other times I thought of myself as marvelously unique. In time, I came to see my life as a bridge, stretched at each end. It reached from the war-shattered streets of Hannover and the mother deprivation of the *Admiral Muir*, all the way to the highest levels of an American Ivy League education.

Our adaptation to American ways was gradual and proceeded on many fronts, but it was never complete. I was the most eager and adept, my father the least. His thoughts and habits lingered in a past from which he could not escape, a lifetime spent elsewhere and with others. Until his death, my father asked for and cooked the cholesterol-laden and onion-heavy foods with which he was familiar. He always judged clothes by the quality of their fabric, which he fingered carefully and could also test with fire and chemicals. Although he eventually learned some English (having spent fifteen years running a business), it was always a tortured process for him. He could not assist himself, as my mother did, with Latin letter-based dictionaries, and the script in which English was written stretched his resources, although he did read it when he had to. Because my sister, after speaking Yiddish as a young child, eventually spoke only English at home, his ear became more alert to the new language as he grew older, although he always spoke Yiddish at home.

I did not help him learn English because I always spoke to him in Yiddish, indulging him in this as in so many other ways. He used me as a *dolmatcher* (translator) for important phone calls and official business (including organizing and typing materials he presented to his tax accountant, Morris Teichman). My mother, whose English was accented, but increasingly wide-ranging and accurate was never good enough for him in these matters; only his American-educated daughter would do. Like so many immigrant children, I served him as a liaison to a world in which he never felt comfort and whose foreign language was there only to trap, confound, and mislead him. I hated doing it, not only did it burden and imprison my childhood in adult responsibilities, but it also exposed his vulnerabilities and inverted the power relations of our household. This made me both painfully uncomfortable and endowed me with competence I did not really feel. My father always maintained control in our house. In this translation business, too, he continued to exercise control over me while also revealing its fatal flaw. Like seeing him on board ship (I saw him only once) incapable of moving or acting, these English language-based incapacities were painful to me in the deepest ways. If my father's failing in English embarrassed him, they were a form of complex shame for me. They exposed him to my own ridicule, which I tried desperately not to feel. In our household, we all worked hard to protect my father from exposure, maintaining a false sense of his control and competence that was revealed most completely when my mother became ill.

One time, however, when my father needed to take his literacy test in order to register to vote, was warm and wonderful. (My mother was already voting; she had had no problem passing the required test.) My father dreaded the testing, but he wanted to participate fully as a citizen and studied the required questions on history, mostly about presidents and government structure. I went with him to the exam room (which happened to be at my own Lefferts Junior High School) and sat outside the classroom while he took the test. He was very nervous when we arrived. After it was over, he asked me one history question about which he was uncertain, and when I confirmed his answer he beamed and said that it wasn't so bad. He knew he had passed and was proud of it. He was then probably in his late fifties. Struggling all the way, he had clearly not stopped growing and in his own difficult way adapting to a new life.

As a result of my role as translator and liaison, I knew all about their business, their German reparations matters, their medical issues. As *dolmatcher*, I absorbed what I heard, while serving technically only as an intermediary. And they knew that they could trust me not to talk about these matters with others. Despite all this knowledge and these complex entanglements, I did not know all their secrets. Even as a child, I saw certain discrepancies. My mother had always said that my father was six years older than she was, but his papers indicated only a one-year difference in age. Only much later, just before he died, when my father told me that he was eighty years old, did I realize that he had kept his age a secret from me all of his life. I never knew why. All those years he had me give his birth date on documents of all kinds as August 25, 1909. In fact, he now proclaimed that he was born in 1903. My parents often discussed people's ages, and many times claimed that this or that individual had shaved off years. It had never occurred to me that my father had done this, too. But at a time when homes, belongings, children, parents were up for grabs, why not also age? When he told me his "real" age, he seemed pleased by my quite genuine surprise. He probably told me only because he wanted me to get it right on the stone after his death.

I had always known that he was old, but never quite how old he really was. He never even looked the age he officially claimed. His dark hair became lightly speckled by grey only in what I now know to have been his early sixties. His face remained largely unlined. He did not wear reading glasses until he was well into his fifties. Only his hands, with which he had worked constantly since his childhood, betrayed him. They trembled ever since I could remember. He could never keep them from shaking when he held them out. It was a sign of his nerves, and he laughed when he showed me how they shook. His hands described an inner state that exposed in their own language his painful frailties.

Of course, his attitudes were always several generations behind the times in which I grew up. Even compared with my friends' parents, those views of my parents, and my father's especially, seemed antediluvian. I attributed this to his being an immigrant from Eastern Europe and a Holocaust survivor, and I excused him for this as a result. I may even have absorbed some of it, as older perspectives allowed me to see as a historian sees, with two sets of eyes. In my view, Holocaust survivors deserved serious leeway for their attitudes, and their sensitivities (even their temper tantrums) required indulgence. My own feelings or understanding usually gave way to his more "acute" understanding of the tragedies of life—more real surely than my own superficial, modern perspectives unforged in tragedy. In fact, my father was out of touch with the world into which I grew, at least in part, because he was born even before many of my friends' grandparents had been born and in a premodern place. He was from an altogether different world, but because his feelings came first in our house, his perspectives were often allowed to dominate even when my mother or I knew better. My father insisted on things that sometimes did not make a lot of sense to my mother, but, because she indulged him and because she insisted that we respect him, that dominance made our household bizarrely composed of elements of different eras. She often had to coax him to see reason and to adapt to current realities.

My initial surprise and puzzlement about my father's age was compounded when I finally got his birth certificate in Lodz. On this "official" document, he is described as having been born on August 1906 (August 20th, but this was clearly incorrect—most likely a transcribing glitch since he had no reason to alter the day). Now I was really in a quandary. Had my father after all those years of misrepresentation simply forgotten how old he really was, transposing a six-year difference to 1903, rather than a three-year difference, which would have been 1906? Did his memory actually fail him in the end? Had I lied on his headstone? I will never really know, though I am far more suspicious of that birth certificate, official-seeming as it is, than of either my father's memory or his ability to calculate. Probably his parents, in fear of Russian officials and possible conscription for their son, had lied when they registered his birth. At least that is my most recent and reasoned conclusion. My father always knew who he was, and it is inconceivable to me that he did not know his real age, although he had no doubt long manipulated it to his advantage as needed. If my father was born in 1903, as seems likely, then he was forty-one when he went to Auschwitz, too old to survive the selection. At that critical juncture in his life, his looks had deceived his age and all his calculations as he watched his sons disappear into the other line. Technically too old to survive this moment of time, he lived finally to almost double that age.

Of course, his age was only the simplest of his secrets. Much deeper secrets troubled him. As a child, privy to his business, I thought I knew them all, and as a child with whom they shared their memories, I thought I also shared their past. In fact, all along my relationship with my father was based on subtle deceptions, deceptions to which I had been complicit. And my knowledge of their past was feeble and incomplete. I helped him believe that he was a powerful presence in an American world where his powers were an illusion. I now realize that I also had created in my mind a powerful figure, critically compromised by his dependence on me-someone who could try to protect me (as he had tried so hard to protect his other children) but who, in the end, needed my knowledge and my skills even to survive in the simpler world of American realities. In my flawed knowledge of his past, I had somehow created memories of him in which my father had heroically saved his children, hidden them, fed them, sheltered them until the very end.

———

There was always anxiety in my house, fears about health and safety, worries about money, suspicions about officials. I did not think of this as unusual. All children, I imagined, waited at the window with their mothers if their fathers were just a few minutes late; all children listened to the sound of their parents breathing when they were sick; all children hid their family secrets (including their political party affiliation) from their friends and neighbors. "Never sign a petition of any kind," my father told me; "never sign a blank piece of paper which could become a debt." My childhood was a bed of anxieties, a diet of anxieties, a wardrobe of anxieties. Today, as I worry about my own children, I realize how much of this is a continuation of my upbringing. Of course, all children worry. Only our innocent concepts of childhood propose it to be worry free. But my childhood had much more worry than most. Only later, as I met friends whose lives were not defined by parents with trembling hands, did I realize that pervasive anxiety was not common to childhood experience; then I began to understand how much this had taken its toll on them, and on me.

Many times my parents' health was an issue—my mother's stomach problems, my father's headaches and asthma. My father had a long bout with sciatica that left him without muscle tone in his right leg and briefly addicted to morphine. At one point, my mother received a call from the police after he was found collapsed at a subway station with a head injury. He had apparently suffered a dizzy spell and fallen over. This was a nightmare come true as I returned from graduate school to meet my mother at his hospital bed. Although he had many subsequent dizzy spells, only once do I recall any basis for real concern about government agents. I was about ten years old, and we had moved by then to the beautiful five-room apartment (with two full bathrooms) in an elevator building not far from my uncle's house and close to the Brooklyn Museum and the Botanical Gardens. My mother had made friends with many of our wonderful neighbors, some of whom had a long communist past and continuing communist beliefs. One day, two FBI agents knocked at our door and introduced themselves. Did we know of any communist activity in the building, they asked. My mother said that she had no knowledge of any such thing. Of course, she knew very well that once a month something like a group met in a kitchen on the third floor of our building (among its members was Herbert Aptheker later to become the head of the American Communist Party). But my mother and father, who themselves never belonged to any party except

the Democratic Party and whose small business instincts made them
wary of communists, would never have told on a friend or neighbor. To
do otherwise, my father once told me with great passion, was the lowest level to which a human being could stoop. Not only did they suspect
officials of all kinds, though their own ultraclean lives would hardly have
made them vulnerable (my father always overpaid his taxes by never
taking anything more than a 10-percent standard deduction despite the
accountant he engaged), but loyalty to each other and to those we knew
was our unspoken creed. We always kept each other's secrets.

We moved when I was in fifth grade to an area of Brooklyn that was
still overwhelmingly white (though I did meet my childhood friend from
Bedford Stuyvesant, Barbara Killens, in junior high school a few years
later). Our new neighborhood had very good schools; my uncle had made
sure of that. The move was evidence of our mobility and meant that my
father's hard work and mother's careful housekeeping had landed us several notches up from where we had started in America. The apartment
we rented was the most spacious and expensive in the whole building.
This was where I really grew up, the place from which I went forth to
attend high school, began to be interested in boys, had a sweet sixteen
party, and began my life at Barnard College. My good friend, Sandra
Leon, who was three years older, lived next door and helped me to grow
up while I helped her to understand history, a subject she simply could
not grasp. Our rooms were on the same fire-escape, just a wall apart.
We had Passover and Thanksgiving celebrations here with my aunt and
uncle in attendance, and on Carroll Street I got an *Encyclopedia Britan-
nica* and a typewriter, learned to write term papers, and to read French.
My parents spent their best years here as my father's business prospered,
we vacationed in the Catskills in the summer, and spent weekends in the
Brooklyn Museum or the Botanical Gardens. My father loved the Egyp-
tology collection at the museum with its real mummies (the best in New
York). We all loved the Botanical Gardens with their hills of daffodils
and alleys of cherry blossoms, Japanese tea garden and fragrant herb

garden for the blind. In the winter the garden was full of clean snow, and a sultry glasshouse was warm with exotic plants and strange orchids. I remember reading *Uncle Tom's Cabin, Citizen Paine,* and many volumes of C. P. Snow on a bench in these gardens and watching the annual contest for Cherry-Blossom Queen. We got our first (Brownie) camera and took pictures of ourselves, often at the Botanical Gardens, then free of any admissions charge and seemingly always open to our needs as a family and as individuals.

We spent wonderful hours together as a family, and I spent hours with my mother as we shopped at the original Loehmann's with its naked marble statue, golden staircase, and the venerable Mrs. Loehmann in residence. It was just a few blocks from our house, down Bedford Avenue. (At Loehmann's everyone undressed amidst the racks and men were strictly confined to the first several feet of the store with its two large gilded chairs.) Loehmann's still had a pneumatic tube that sent payments and change from the downstairs to the elegant designer evening section upstairs. My mother and I had similar clothing tastes, and we often found each other with the same item in our hands. My mother shopped sparingly, but still retained her eye both for the well-designed clothing item and a sense of good value. Loehmann's was then a mecca for really good clothes at low prices. It was much more fun than downtown Brooklyn department stores, where my mother and I shopped mainly at May's and Abraham and Strauss.

In the third year we lived on Carroll Street, my mother spent two weeks at Mt. Sinai Hospital where she underwent a hysterectomy and had a benign lump removed from her breast. My father, who completely distrusted surgeons and hospitals, was terrified and beside himself. He actually confronted the very able and well-known gynecologist (Dr. Berglass) after my mother was wheeled out of surgery looking like death. "What have you done to the mother of two children?" he yelled in a combination of Yiddish and English. She recovered very well, although she never did have the follow-up visits or hormone-replacement treatments

The Botanical Gardens in Brooklyn was a haven for my family throughout the year. In this winter photo, my sister, Iris Marsha Fass, and I are playing with the snow posing with my father. The photo is probably from 1958.

that she should have. My mother feared going to doctors almost as much as my father did and put off such visits in order to avoid bad news. She always had a variety of digestive problems and neglected a long-standing gall bladder condition (first diagnosed in Germany when she was pregnant with me). In the long run this haunted her life and mine. But she had not been able to ignore the extraordinary uterine bleeding that summer we spent in the Catskills. Her friend Bella Koss urged her to seek help. When she finally did, she was sent to the hospital immediately after seeing the doctor. Because my mother was in the hospital at the time, she

This photograph shows my sister, Iris Marsha Fass, my father, and me during spring blossom time in the Botanical Gardens. It is probably also from 1958.

was not able to take my sister to her first day at school, something she long regretted. By the time she had fully recovered at home, my sister, always a quick study, could read, which startled her and made her delight in Iris's achievement but feel miserable about her absence.

When we lived on Carroll Street my mother's circle of friends began to expand well beyond the group of survivors whom she had known. She made friends easily with neighbors in the large apartment building where we lived, and all over the street, as well as with other mothers at school. She always attended school events and joined the PTA. She was extremely well liked and would chat in her melodious voice in an English in which she was rapidly becoming quite accomplished. All the shop-keepers along DeKalb Avenue where we still shopped at small specialty stores respected her. Here there were two European bakeries, two deli-catessens, a butter and cheese store, a herring and pickle store that also sold dried fruits and mushrooms, a fresh fruit and vegetable store, a fish store, and several kosher butchers. She ran an excellent household, began to adopt American foods into her repertoire (I remember fresh orange juice and broiled meats), and dropped some of the older more leaden and fatty Yiddish foods like *kishka*. My mother was always eager to learn things of all kinds, and she astonished me with her increasing knowledge about nutrition and decorating. She was always busy, but never tired, and she glowed through her identification with my academic achievements. Her pleasure on parents' nights when she met my teachers was obvious, and she started the ritual of making contributions into the little *pushka* (box for charity) before each of my exams. These were growing in num-ber and variety (ordinary tests and quizzes, finals, Regents exams, SATs). It seemed to work very well.

When my father was reluctant to send me to a college for which he had to pay tuition when I could go to a very good place like Brooklyn College for free and insisted that his views about this were correct, she persuaded him that Barnard was worth the money. She may well have offered to reduce her own allowance in return. My mother always approached things in a much more reasonable and far quieter manner than my father, whose outbursts of passion and determination punctu-ated our lives. But both she and he drew the line at my going to a college to which I could not commute. Vassar, a college I long dreamed about, was off limits, although we did try at one point to figure out how long it might take for me to get there by train each day. Barnard, an hour away by subway (it was one and a half hours after we moved to Sheepshead Bay) was fine. For an inflexible man who always insisted on making the decisions, my father was remarkably persuadable. My mother never needed to seem to exercise control, but her simple, rational appeals, always made in a low, unharassing voice, usually did the trick. She did it once again when, despite my father's sharp objections, she urged me to take the job at Berkeley in California that I was offered in 1974. This would seriously separate me from them for the first time. I remember very well the conversation around our glass-topped wrought-iron kitchen table when I laid out the possibilities this offer might bring me and suggested that I would stay in the New York area if this is what they wanted. No, my mother insisted, "at some point the baby bird has to leave the nest, and the hardest thing for the mother bird to do is to push her baby out." She died three years later.

———

Looking back, I now associate the last house we all lived in together with her death. But at the time we moved, just before my junior year in college, this was a very happy event. As the one and only house they ever owned, it both frightened and excited them. Though well located in the Sheepshead Bay area of Brooklyn, close to the marina (where we later loved to walk) and Manhattan Beach, it meant a longer trip for my father to work, a very long commute for me to Barnard, and for my sister a complicated trip to Madison High School where she enrolled. But it proved both a good investment and a very nice location. My mother and I went to clean it and to lay down contact paper in all of its many kitchen cupboards. We brought bread and salt with us that first day, in the traditional East European Jewish manner of welcome. There was already a *mezzuza* on the front door. We marveled at the dishwasher (soon to break) and the large front porch, although we were less pleased to now be reduced to just one and one-half bathrooms. We discussed how we would furnish it—carpeting, drapes, flooring in the hall. We already had a Knoll dining room set (with a 1950s feel that my mother never liked), but we needed lots of other new furnishings.

Over the next several years, the house was created according to my mother's tastes (except for the left-over dining room). We had beautiful gold wool pile carpeting in the living room and up the stairs, and a large Kerman patterned Karistan rug in the dining room. My mother and I refinished the wood floor ourselves. She found lovely, hand-embroidered French panels, which she ordered and had made up for the public rooms; she had to search these out because no one else was using them yet in those drape-heavy days, but she remembered them from her merchandizing and refused to settle for the machined imitations. She bought a silk, three-piece celadon-colored sofa with a hand-made frame, small, carved Italian ladies chairs, and a lovely Italian-style upright piano in cherry. Even before we moved into the house, my mother had eyed and finally purchased a splendid, thick grey-veined-marble-topped mahogany coffee table which we brought with us. Finally, she bought an antique reproduction Empire knick-knack cabinet to display the objects we had brought over in barrels from Germany. She spent weeks and months getting things set up just right. The effect was elegant and serene (never ornate as was the style those days), and my mother seemed to have fulfilled a dream.

My mother and I did some of the shopping together (we spotted the chairs in the window one day after the store was already closed), but even when I did not shop with her for every object, she always waited for my approval before she bought it. As a result of my snobbish disapproval of anything "kitcheny," they wound up with an enormous and very heavy wrought iron set for the dining area of the kitchen, complete with a round glass-topped table. It was so unwieldy that cleaning around it (or walking around it) was difficult. (Maybe I sought out a round table where there would be no head; still, my father always sat in one place, at the extreme right, where no one else was allowed to sit.) It was around this table that so many important decisions were made: whom and when my sister married; my decision to go to Berkeley; my father's reluctant agreement to go to Israel with my mother for their twenty-fifth anniversary. Also around this table my mother and I spoke late into the night when I came home from graduate school and later from my first job at Rutgers University. Here I asked her for the names of the five children, which I kept safely hidden in my passport case until I went to Poland. This table defined our family space, special in its nestlike coziness, though heavy with black wrought-iron. It was also here that we watched television on a small set, when the TV was banished from our now uninhabitable "living room"—the room which lived only as an expression of my mother's imagination.

For the first time, my sister and I didn't share a bedroom. Each of us had a good-sized room facing the backyard, which my father cultivated with flowering bushes like peonies, and Japanese maples, roses, and tomato vines. He wanted to grow potatoes, but my mother stopped him. Each of us had bookshelves and red wall-to-wall carpeting, and I got a new bedroom set (which I still have and use). But not long after we moved into this place, I moved out, finally to live on my own (so to speak) when I went to graduate school at Columbia University. I experienced only then (at twenty), what many of my friends did when they went off as college freshmen (and I had dreamed of), an existence separate and apart from my parents.

My separation came differently than planned. I had expected to spend a year in Germany on the Fulbright Fellowship I had been awarded and then to go on to Harvard to study history with the help of a Woodrow Wilson grant. All these plans had been set, and I was two weeks away from boarding the USS *Constitution* for my first view of Germany since early 1951, when I became aware that my father was withdrawn and seemed to have lost weight and energy. He was clearly deeply troubled, though I had until then either not noticed or ignored it. I asked my mother if it was related to my plans to spend the year away in Germany. "Of course," she said, "he has been sick about it." My father, my mother, and I sat down at the round wrought-iron kitchen table and talked. What was wrong I wanted to know. "Was it related to my plans to go to Europe for a year?" "Of all places you could have chosen," my father said, "why Germany?" He said this calmly and sadly, not in a fit of passion or pique. For many years, I had been telling people that I was an immigrant from Germany (so much more acceptable than admitting to roots in Poland) that I had managed to deceive myself into believing that in going to Germany it would be a kind of return home. But, as soon as he spoke I knew instantly what he meant. I realized that we had never discussed this decision that I alone had made. "Of course," I told him, "I will not go." His relief and excitement were palpable. My mother too was deeply relieved, though her emotions were much less obvious. "But what will you do," he asked? "I will work it out," I replied.

During that long day I informed the steamship company, the Fulbright Commission, and the Federal Republic of Germany. I, however, was left in early June 1967 without any plans for the next year. The next day I called Columbia, a familiar institution, an almost homelike place, located in not-so-far-away Manhattan. Because the Graduate Faculties had admitted me into its history program, they had no problem doing so again, but they could not promise me any kind of financial support. I had the great good luck on that same day to recoup the lucrative four-year New York State Lehmann Fellowship I had rejected just two months earlier when I had made other plans. In those two days I gained a telephone confidence I never knew I had as I negotiated to rescue myself and my parents from a set of foolish plans I had somehow imagined could become my own. How could I, the child of these parents, propose to go off to Freiburg, Germany, (of all places), to study Freud's German reception in the 1920s and then return to leave them once again as I went off to Cambridge, Massachusetts. It was clear to me that not even my college degree had made my parents like other parents—proud of their child's achievement and ready to part with her—nor had it made me simply a second-generation American like others. I had hoped someday to outgrow or outwit my difference from everyone else. By the time I was twenty, I knew otherwise.

Instead of Germany for a year, my father agreed that I could go to Europe and Israel for a long summer (three months) as a graduation gift.

They were clearly ready now to part with me in this modest and limited way; my father was even eager to sponsor and support it. I promised that it would cost very little money as I pondered my *Europe on $5 A Day* and found an inexpensive charter flight on Sabena Airlines. I left very shortly after graduation, initially coordinating my trip with two other Barnard seniors. It was an extraordinary experience, a summer of freedom and adventure in which my mother and I exchanged long letters in German. Hers were delivered to an American Express office everywhere I went—England, Holland, France, Italy, Switzerland, and Belgium. Only in Israel were the letters delivered to the houses of my relatives where I stayed. I never set foot in Germany.

Still, I did leave the house after that summer when I went to graduate school at Columbia, and in leaving I lost a sense of their day-to-day existence. I imagined they were happy. They had friends nearby, including my mother's good friend from Hannover, Bella Koss, who now lived less than two blocks away. Initially, my sister was still at home. I spoke to them regularly, probably every day, and I thought we were very close. I spent many weekends at home with them. I followed all the details about their health, kept up with news about their friends. I heard about my mother's plans for the house, about my uncle's health. I told my parents, my mother especially, about my experiences and thought this made her life more satisfying. And for a while they did live almost normal lives. My sister was growing up; her boyfriends lined up on the front porch. But after my sister moved to Barnard College and then married while still at school, their lives began to shrink, and their social interactions thinned. (My mother put a huge, elaborate basket of carefully arranged dolls in my sister's empty room. Neither my sister nor I had ever been especially fond of dolls, but my mother treasured them.) And then after my father retired in 1970 and began to take control of the household and my mother's daily life, the quality of their lives very much changed for the worse. My father always needed to keep busy, and now that activity came at her expense. By 1973, I came home from either New Jersey or later Kennedy

Airport, spent a few days, and then left them there together at the edge
of sidewalk where they looked small. I was so glad they had each other,
and I thought they were happy.

Not until I had lived for a year or so in California and returned for a
visit did I realize how unhappy my mother had become (and what a sac-
rifice it must have been to let me go). One evening in our kitchen corner
she began to cry as she told me how he was restricting her life and confin-
ing her movements. She wanted to do volunteer work or take courses, but
he objected. He went with her everywhere when she shopped. My father's
combination of dependence and explosive self-assertion had been bear-
able when the children were still around, but, now left alone with him,
she realized how truly mismated they were. "He is consuming my life,"
she cried.

I was shocked. I had always known they were deeply different but
thought of them as bound together by Auschwitz, and I assumed that
since she had allowed him to dominate in everything that she acquiesced
in his control. I told her to do what she wanted, that she didn't need his
permission. (I had, after all, left.) I even told her to divorce him. My
own independence, dearly bought, now made me bold. But that was
simply neither real nor possible to her. Instead, in the two years that
had included my uncle's death and my move to California, she began to
yield to the disease that had been long festering inside her. I have always
pictured it this way—she fended off the growth in her gall-bladder and
in the narrow bile duct into which it drained (and that finally killed her)
as long as others needed her—my uncle's illness, my sister's increasingly
problematic marriage, my career. And then when my father and she
became ever more alone and he gave her no room to grow or dream,
when his past overshadowed everything in its path, she gave vent to the
frustrations of a lifetime of personal denial, and she let the bile take
over. The bile—yellow and brown, thick and thin—contained her anger
(never expressed), her pain usually hidden, her disappointments and
regrets, and her memories. And this settled inside her and finally killed

her. When she lay dying in her bedroom upstairs on the new single mattress I finally insisted she needed in order to die in greater autonomy, she asked in semidelirium, but quite calmly, "Who are the Hasidim gathered around the bed?" This I understood was her past come back, a past she always fended off through sheer force of will bound up in her ample goodness. My mother had believed in life and tried to grab onto an unfolding future, but the past remained ready to pounce.

During the nine months after her surgery in April 1977, after they discovered the inoperable cancer of the bile duct, we lived hopelessly all together in the house on East 27th Street (even my sister and her husband moved in). My mother was pretty much completely confined to the house; aside from medical visits, she left it only twice: Once she tested her strength on a very brief walk; again on Yom Kippur she insisted, "If I am alive, I will walk to the synagogue." She fasted the whole day. She was testing herself, again, I think, and realized just how sick she was.

During this period of increasing bitterness for all of us, we realized that she had always held us together. I had taken leave from the university (the gift of a wonderful chairman, and later friend, Bob Middlekauff), to tend to her, to rent taxis to go to upper Manhattan for radiation treatments at Columbia Presbyterian Hospital where she had her surgery, to talk to her doctor, to dress her festering wound through which bile flowed into a colostomy bag. The doctors knew it was hopeless and told us so. Her surgeon, Dr. Markowitz, had literally concocted a method during the surgery as a temporary drain for her bile to keep her alive while her cancer continued to grow. She might otherwise have died on the operating table. She had been in surgery for more than six hours for what we had expected to be an operation of two or, at most, three, and my father and I, waiting together, did not know what to think and imagined the worst. In the hospital before and after the surgery she kept the book I had just published at her bedside (I still had only the one first copy which I had given to them), showing anyone who stopped by, her daughter's latest achievement. On the subway train to her hospital one morning, I discovered a review in the *New York Times* when I saw my own photo at the top of the second section, staring me in the face. It was unexpected, and at any other time the review would have been the source of ecstatic delight. It pleased my mother but felt like lead to me. I was in despair, bargaining with God. After three weeks in the hospital, she came home only to need to return every weekday to 168th Street in Manhattan for radiation treatments. We did not own a car, and this meant hiring a cab to take us back and forth. On the long trip home she was always very, very ill. We saw a little improvement as she recovered from the surgery itself. I found out about an experimental chemotherapy treatment at the Sloan Kettering Cancer Center, where she went once and became part of a medical protocol. Neither the radiation nor the chemotherapy could change the facts of her disease, while she expended her energies and time riding back and forth in taxicabs. After a long and painful conversation with her surgeon, I stopped the treatments, for which she was grateful. On one of my trips to California I tried to find out about alternative therapies from hippies in the Bay area. Mostly, my mother and I talked, and I counted the days we had left together. She asked if she was dying, and I could not tell her the truth because my father had forbidden it. Over time, the pain became unbearable, and because she was at home in prehospice days no one could give her adequate pain medication (she took Tylenol with codeine orally). Her doctors prescribed antibiotics for her frequent and ever-more debilitating fevers. The bile flowed brown and yellow by turns.

Three times during those nine months I ran away, back to California to be alone and to treasure my own space. Each time, I returned fearing that she might already have died. My father would call and tell me that I had to come home right away, and I left the next day. The final time, when my father called at four in the morning, I took the first plane out of San Francisco, aching to see her alive just one more time. I wrote a poem for her on the airplane to pass the time. She waited. When I entered the room in the dark on her birthday (February 1), she heard me immediately and uttered her last words, "Honey, honey, honey, your voice is like honey. Your life should be as sweet." I sat all night in the big lounge chair my father had moved into the bedroom. She died early the next morning. We were all there.

A few weeks earlier she had insisted that we bring Mr. Cohen, an orthodox Jewish man who lived two houses down from us, to see her. She entrusted him with her wishes, which we were meant to overhear, "Just a plain pine box, and a religious burial supervised by an Orthodox Jewish funeral home." She probably didn't trust us any more because we had lied to her about the seriousness of her disease (my father had even insisted that her surgeon not tell her she had cancer). During the entire nine months, the word cancer was never uttered in the house. My father had forbidden it. She too had initially been eager to believe that the fake stones in a jar that my brother-in-law (a medical intern) provided was the source of her disease. She had gall stones and nothing more. But after months of fevers and infections and then agonizing pain that never went away, she knew. She told me that it was worse than childbirth but without the hoped-for happy ending. And then, after she saw her Hasidim, she stopped talking to my father altogether. She would not take the antibiotics to keep the infection in check, and she stopped eating. She literally shut her teeth to any attempts to pass anything into her mouth. It was the hardest part of my life, harder than our initial separation on board the *Admiral Muir*, harder than trying to separate from her as an adolescent at college, harder than childbirth. I sat *shiva* for the full seven days, then walked around the block with my father on a frigid February day with frozen snow everywhere. (The earth had been so hard that they almost couldn't dig the grave to bury her the day after she died.) I left him there alone in the house she had designed and returned to Berkeley. My mother and I, I thought, were now both free.

———

I loved both my parents all my life, but as a child I adored my father and preferred him as a role model. I thought him better looking and more authoritative then my mother. I have no memory of him in Germany and only remember communicating with him in Yiddish in America. Maybe he was always a bit mysterious to me and therefore intriguing. He never talked much and never ever hit me (a point of pride and principle), but his disapproving glance was enough of a warning. Probably this sense of his power made him so attractive. Later, I thought of his power in different terms, and by the time my mother died, I equated it with tyranny.

I realized later that this was a mistake. My father was extremely dependent on my mother and appreciated her talents and character. His strength was actually more superficial than hers. While he could be overtly bellicose and tried to rule through tantrums, he also had a soft side and he was far more yielding than he wanted anyone to know. On the surface, however, my mother was always the pacifist, seemingly dependent upon him.

His objection to going to Israel was a perfect example of this pattern. My sister, her husband, and I had planned it as a twenty-fifth wedding anniversary gift and a surprise. The trip was arranged for June in time for their anniversary. When we broke the news to them, the surprise was on us. Because he had not made the decision, he became hostile and intransigent in his rejection of the plan. Despite our pleading—my mother's, mine, my sister's and her husband's—he refused to budge. He was simply not going. Then he took his hat and his overcoat and left the house. We were aghast; my mother was in tears. How could he be so unreasonable? In about half an hour he returned and asked to see the tickets. Well, "what's done is done," he proclaimed. The tickets were paid for. They would go.

I agreed to stay and watch over the house during the three weeks of their absence, collect the mail (essential to his peace of mind), pay the bills, and so on. He returned looking like a prince; his then-silvering hair had grown long and curled at the bottom. He was tanned and handsome. They had had a wonderful time. He had seen his family and even taken a bunch of pictures with a camera we had given him before he left. As I reflect today on that experience, it is clearer to me that part of the problem was my father's unwillingness to let anyone else make decisions for him, but another was his suspicion of anything that smacked of planned enjoyment. He punished himself all his life and thus also punished those around him who shared his life.

The trip to Israel was the one and only time my mother went anywhere by plane, even though she was adventurous, loved to travel, and had no fear of flying. She looked forward to the adventure. But my father would fly again, although he was afraid of flying and, as I increasingly understood, of lots of other things. He returned to Israel a few years after my mother died to retrieve my aunt and also brought back the picture of his first family. He could now face them again. And he flew to San Francisco immediately after he was told that my daughter Bluma (Bibi), the only grandchild he would ever know, was born. He arrived the same day. Such an event was just too important to miss.

Later, when he was alone (I had left him very much alone after my mother died), he might have had lots of opportunities to meet other women, but he told me that he drew the line at two wives. Maybe he understood that he was too hard to live with and his deeper kindness made him decide to spare another wife. He certainly longed to take care of someone, to give of himself as he had provided for others all his life. This is what probably helped him to decide to offer his new home (a walk-up apartment just down the street from the house he had once owned and sold after my mother died) to my Tante Fela when she was completely crippled and her Alzheimer's already well progressed. Maybe he was trying to compensate for his failure to give enough of this kindness to my mother. At the time, I saw it as sheer guilt, but I was then still gripped by the pain of my identification with my mother, my anger at him, and the unquenchable loss I felt after her death. I wish now that I had been able to be more forgiving. After all, most of my life I had tried to understand and protect him. Only this time, my anger got the upper hand. After my mother died, I left him to his own resources in ways that I never had before and never would have imagined I could.

He made all the arrangements for the sale of the house and his move for himself. My sister's own deteriorating home life left her useless. I was a continent away. He gathered his energy and carefully packed up all my mother's precious objects, reassembling them in the new apartment. The silk on the sofa had begun to split. He saved what he could of the furniture, but he bought a new sleeper sofa bed for my husband and me to use when we came to visit. When my aunt moved in he gave her the large bedroom and the double bed. He moved into the narrow second bedroom, which contained only a bed and the old Grundig hi fi and shortwave (in shiny mahogany) that he had proudly bought years before. Here alone in a largely bare room, my father slept, and it was here we put the playpen in which my daughter slept when we visited him in Brooklyn. My father and she shared a room, and he played with his one and only grandchild when she woke early in the morning. He had always been an early riser, and he was already awake when Bibi woke up. The details are almost too painful to recollect. He never imagined that he would have grandchildren, and I suppose this unexpected pleasure was something that he could accept and enjoy. I was, by then, always criticizing him—for drinking too much coffee or not dusting well enough, not taking care of himself. But he cooked for himself and my aunt and us when we came, and he shopped and cleaned and did the laundry. I knew that he would do things his own way, listening with one ear only as I spoke with half a heart.

There came a time when, my life having blossomed and my sense of obligation returned, we finally planned to spend a half year (an academic leave) on the East Coast in order to be near him. He had by then spent almost seven years without my mother, not exactly by himself, but very much alone. Then in the midst of our planning he died. We got a phone call at six in the morning on a Sunday. I knew immediately that it was bad news. The policeman told me that he was sorry but that my father had "passed away." They had found him dead in the narrow bed in the second floor apartment. (During the weeks before this he had told me about his shortness of breath and his fatigue; he also confessed his real age.) I responded instantly to the police officer that there was to be no autopsy. When he insisted that this was required because he had died of "unknown causes," I replied with ever greater vigor, "no autopsy, my father was a religious Jew." My father had always feared "the knife," and I would protect him from it now. We made all the arrangements to return, and I discussed with my sister instructions about removing jewelry, calling the funeral home, and informing friends.

I saw him for the last time in his casket (a plain pine box). He was wrapped in his woolen *talit* (prayer shawl). He was born a Jew, suffered as a Jew, and died as a Jew. He was waxen and his mouth was open, maybe he tried for a last breadth as his heart gave out, or for a last laugh as he finally faced God. I kissed his very cold forehead and said goodbye.

By his reckoning he was eighty-one years old. By the reckoning of his citizenship papers he was seventy-five, and by that of the birth certificate I obtained in Poland he was seventy-eight. By anyone's calculations, he

This is the last photograph I have of me and my father, taken in July 1983.

had lived a long and very difficult life. I missed him immediately and ever more as time passed.

———

Many of the things I learned as a child about my parents' lives seemed to contain some kind of secret, and it was assumed that most things I knew about us and our lives were to be kept strictly as private knowledge— their finances, the amount of their reparations payments, the bank safety-deposit box where they hid their home insurance documents, citizenship papers, and my mother's jewelry. There were also the secret diamonds, which my father told me he had hidden in Lodz before the war. I now know that there were many things that were also kept from me. My father's age, the names of the dead children and their ages, Chelmno to which so many of their loved ones went, the photo of my father's family, the fate of Tante Brandel's husband in Russia. And the fate of the children that he hid from the Nazis, a fate he may have tried to hide from himself. Things that now seem trivial and those that seem profound were equally covert knowledge. Even their political party affiliation as Democrats was to remain a secret. Maybe they hid secrets from each other, but I doubt this because each needed to trust and confide in someone. Despite their many differences, their secrets bound them together. Above all, their deadliest secret was the heinous past they shared, a past in which they had been deprived of everything, everyone, and every possibility of effective action, everything except the detailed memories. It has not been easy to rid myself of this profound commitment to privacy as I write about them. Other people's lives and the human personality itself are, by their nature, shrouded in secret places, and, as Henry James knew, our social life is full of knowing deception. But my parents lived as if they feared being overheard, and sometimes it seemed almost as if their secrets kept them alive. Their experiences had probably deprived them of any real faith, but their new lives had provided them with occasions to reclaim the power of secrets.

The lives of Eastern European Jews, even before the Shoah, were unusually burdened by attempts to hide the self, the family, the Torah and its service, the community, and any important knowledge relating to these. When the Nazis arrived, everything was exposed as Jews were stripped of their possessions and materially, socially, physically, and psychologically *ausgetrieben* (driven out). For most Jews, there was literally no place to hide. They tried to hide some possessions, but these were always found out, as my father discovered in his *sorterei*. They could not even hide their own nakedness as the Nazis deloused them and showered them together. Probably this exposure was quite deliberate since in the Nazi's paranoia and their obsession with the omniscient state, the Jews were, by the nature of their separate history, the most intransigent enemy, knowable only through their genetic code.

For centuries, in their largely self-contained communities throughout Europe the Jews had shown to others only their shared communal identity and little else. They kept their own names, often unpronounceable to their Polish or Russian or Ukrainian neighbors. When I was in Poland, my guide Henrik, told me that the Poles called all the Jews "Mordechai, " a name the Poles despised, and that they gagged and spit when they tried to pronounce it. I suspect that this had little to do with the fact that this was the name of mythical Queen Esther's cousin and everything to do with the "ch" sound—often used in Yiddish, and pronounced not as in Charles but as in Chanukah. This sound, though not altogether unknown to Poles (as it is to Americans), is still a distinctly Yiddish sound. How ironic, therefore, that Mordechai should also hide the Hebrew word "chai" which means life.

For centuries, and in Eastern Europe longer than elsewhere, the Jews lived separate lives, different in dress, language, food, holiday celebrations, ritual, calendar, habits of life, and beliefs. Much of this grew from their religious separation, but some of it also developed its own cultural momentum: so that even nonreligious Jews followed distinct cultural patterns. Thus, despite their long residence, Jews remained a nation apart. Although much of this was self-chosen, it was strongly reinforced by anti-Semitism. In the nineteenth century, when Western European Jews began to join the mainstream or part of the civic space, developments in many parts of Eastern Europe continued to keep the Jews apart and even reinforced their habits of secrecy. The strong exclusionary laws enforced by a tyrannical Russian autocracy especially aggravated relationships between Jews and their neighbors and kept Jews from participating fully in a changing economic, cultural, and social life. Laden with special taxes and other disabilities, Jews were denied the most fundamental rights and had little part to play in the civil society, while Jewish families lived in dread of a draft that took their sons away for decades and from which most never returned. By being left in fear of the public, civil world, symbolized by the draft and represented by government actions, the Jews of Eastern Europe remained far behind those in the West. But even there, Jews maintained their secrets. This commitment to hiding the self no doubt supplied much of the energy that charged European Jewish humor; as Freud explained, humor always tries to uncover, to trick out secrets, and to undeceive.

Where the tsar had failed, the Nazi conquest of the Jewish soul succeeded both by stripping Jews of a common life they could control and by literally outing all European Jews, even those who no longer hid themselves entirely from public life, the minority of assimilated Jews in Eastern Europe and the larger group of those assimilated in Western Europe. It outed them from hiding places in France where even civil status could not protect them; it outed them in Germany as racial laws undercut their conversion to Christianity or the baptism of their children. It found them in Denmark, Holland, and Greece. Hitler found them most easily in Poland, where they lived in the millions. Here the German SS could scoop them up in their small towns and city ghettos, and with only a bit more effort find those, like my mother's family, who had made a home for themselves in the more modern integrated parts of the city. Wherever Hitler came, the Jews were driven out and exposed.

In Lodz, my father, who had been born under the Russian tsar and inherited the habits of his ancestors (and whose parents had probably deceived Polish official registers about the date of his birth), tried to hide his family. Whether he succeeded did not matter (except after he survived and they did not), but he drew upon all the knowledge of the ghetto and its culture to try to dig his children deep into some Polish cave where they would not be found. He dug potatoes for their survival and tried to bury diamonds for whatever might come after the war. For people who were often accused of shunning labor in the ground, my father had plenty of experience with the rough earth. Hiding and secrets were how Jews survived or, in this case, did not survive.

My parents had acted within the limits of their knowledge, of their circumstances, and of their history, virtuously and reasonably. But they had lost their children all the same. Moral action based on historical experience can also create distortions in our behavior in different contexts and times. When we came to the United States, my parents faced a different world with the habits and the chilling knowledge of their past. In the land of transparency, my parents also shielded themselves and their children with secrets. In so doing, their anxieties became our mother's milk. And their secrets? They shared some of these with me; others I overheard in the Yiddish-German-Polish world that I learned to understand when I was young. I learned about their finances and reparations payments as the pretax-preparer-typist-telephone person who connected them to the outside world. Some secrets I will never know and probably have no right to know. My sister was not so lucky. Born in the United States, without access to the many languages of secret knowledge, with educated skills already preempted by an older sibling, and born with a sweet, direct nature that knew no secrets and told everyone about anything she knew (and more), my sister was kept from the hiding places and thereby also became separated from things that were deeply important.

I became a historian. I tried to root out secrets from the cave of the past by digging a different soil from my father, perhaps hoping to find and to resuscitate the children he had not succeeded in saving. Historians know instinctively that much of life is hidden, that what we see today grew out of the buried past, like the greens on root vegetables. For us the ultimate mystery is not God, but the unknowable-but-must-be-understood that preceded us. Historians know that we walk on sacred grounds, often literally as on the Jewish rot of Chelmno. And we learn that we build toward destruction. Some people become historians because they learn about the past in school, others because they live through memory experiences they have inherited and cannot forget. This memoir is the result of my mother's knowledge and the secrets she shared with me.

CHAPTER 7

MY MOTHER/MYSELF

My mother and I were very close, so close that when I began to write this memoir I assumed it was more about her than about me. I now realize that this was an illusion, her life and mine were distinct and separate, and I could never compensate for the loss of her past. At best, I can reconstruct it haltingly and tentatively based on what she told me, what I learned from books, and what I experienced myself. Still, because almost everything I knew about her past, much of what I know about my father's past, and a great deal of my memories of my own childhood are filtered through her stories, this book is hers as well as mine. I now also know there were many stories that she did not tell me. And although her final illness caused me what I thought of as limitless pain, there were dimensions of pain in her life that I not only never experienced but that she also never hinted at. Because we were very close, I can only assume that she faced this pain almost entirely by herself, sharing it with no one. But since all history is only partial history, all memoir is also partial and incomplete.

My relationship with my mother was as complex as it was close. For years, I ran from identifying with her, and I preferred to see myself as my father's child, much as she had preferred her father to her mother; sometimes I identified with my grandmother about whom she had complex feelings. After she died, when one of my colleagues, the late Robert Brentano, asked me what she was like and if I resembled her, I said, "Yes, very much," now acknowledging what had long been apparent to others. There are times now when I look into a mirror and see her face, not precisely, but closely enough, just as she once walked into a local bakery with a wall-sized mirror and yelled out "Mamashe" because she thought she saw her own mother there. Mothers and daughters spend a lifetime in this dance of mutual recognition, which involves steps in both directions.

One of my earliest memories, a memory firmly placed in Germany, of which I have only very few real memories, concerning a conversation I had with my mother about the children who had been taken away. "Will they take me, too," I asked. "No, never," she replied. She spoke with conviction, and I was reassured. My growing strengths drew heavily on her constant reassurances, but the fragility of life still lingered. Of course, no one ever did take me away (except for that seemingly endless time aboard the *Admiral Muir*). My parents spent their lifetimes in anxious protection. I also spent considerable time protecting them and myself— hours of worry that they would die and many secret hours searching for the space where I could glimpse a life apart from the Holocaust. I found this in an American past. In the United States, Jews had lived and died in peace without gas, ovens, and the knowledge of lost children.

My sense of obligation to the past came from my obligation to my mother. This is how I became a historian, but for most of my life I was a historian of things that were not hers. I had separated myself from her by adopting a history of which she had not been part and making this my history. This history was my secret life.

If my American past eventually provided a separate perspective from that of my parents, then during most of my childhood my perspective reflected someone outside of America. I had grown in that marshy substance where the memory of disaster was only partially replaced by the firmer ground of our adopted land. I was deeply different than my contemporaries, unlike them in many ranges of experiences. I often identified with my mother's perspective on things and found many of my peers' lives frivolous. She and I had similar tastes, which did not always coincide with those of my contemporaries. I never had grandparents or cousins I could play with, and I was therefore often alone, far more than other children of the 1950s. I spoke different languages at home. I often felt older, more burdened, and separated from the life around me. Above all, my life was never uncomplicated, and it required a delicate negotiation between my life at home and my life in the rest of America.

This life came at a cost and left a guilty residue. Just as my father had tried to hide his children, I often tried to hide my parents. My love for them was great, my anxiety for their health and well-being, if possible, even greater. But they were painfully old-fashioned and odd in the American context; in their experiences and habits they were more like the grandparents of the other children I knew while growing up. I spoke with them willingly and happily at home in their various foreign tongues, mostly Yiddish. But outside the house, this language made me cringe, and I feared that we would be overheard. My mother once observed that people who spoke French, or Spanish, or Russian never seemed to be ashamed of their foreign language the way Yiddish speakers were. And she was right. There was an archaic quality about Yiddish that could not be explained through mere foreignness. It defined us as historical outsiders as well as refugees and immigrants. So, I set about dividing my life with a sharp scalpel, carefully suturing the edges. I lived a double life and developed a double consciousness, even a double sensibility. There were eruptions: When one of my friends called my father "your old man" in the style of the 1960s, I was irate and told him that it was a terrible insult and never to call my father that again. When my mother wanted to stop to speak with the dean of the Graduate Faculties at the reception after I received my Columbia Ph.D., I told her it was time to leave. Such possible infections around the boundaries of the divide made me nervous. I loved my parents, but I also loved the self I learned to become apart from them.

They brought with them a past I also tried to isolate. It was an inconvenient past in the American context—full of painful inadequacies. My mother loved her Polish past, bruising as it was. Poland had always frightened me. It was a place of death camps, ghettos, and hateful churches; it was a backward country, class-ridden and anti-Semitic. Technologically it was still part of the nineteenth century. Even Western European societies had provided their people with indoor plumbing and hot and cold running water at a time when Polish girls, my mother among them, still hauled water from the *hoyv* (yard) and boys slept on the shelf of the oven/hearth as my father had. Poland embarrassed me. After being in the United States for a number of years, I preferred to say that I was from Germany, though I knew that German beastliness had been the source of my parents' pain, an enormous Jewish grief, and, only through a fault in history, my unexpected birth. Germany was always well regarded despite it all. Even after the disgusting postwar discoveries, Americans still respected Germany. It had science, music, technology, literature. What did Poland have that I could look upon with pride? My mother told me often about Copernicus, Chopin, and Madam Curie, but these seemed to me hardly very Polish. And even in benighted Poland, we Jews were despised. I fled from Poland, frozen by the thought of the possibilities if I had been born there, as my siblings had.

I learned as a child that history was very important and that we had an obligation to know and tell it in all its nastiness. Yet, I turned to a lighter history, the history of another continent, to relieve the agony and to free me of that other past. America was an opportunity for self-creation and a means to use one history to rectify another. When we were called to be interviewed by the American consul in Hannover, after we applied to immigrate, the official there told my mother that "America is a country for your daughter. It is a land in which she can grow and develop opportunities. The future will be hers." I was told this story as a child, and I used it to leverage my rights to America. The history that had created me I rejected; rather, I embraced a better past, imperfect for sure, but in all ways more appropriate to the future I fantasized and sought. I became an American, a successful American, by adopting not the American present (which always seemed at least partly strange to the divided me) but the

American past, which I could learn as well, or perhaps even better, than children born here. History could be studied and known by historians no matter what their particular personal pasts. In fact, I had something of an advantage by seeing it from a perspective on the margins, as I felt myself to be, at an angle that was slightly askew. In this way, I could notice things that others took for granted and ask questions that revealed cultural patterns so ingrained they were hardly observable to others.

My mother never objected. She must have understood. She always "protected" what she called "your studies," even from bad news, such as my uncle's impending death. As a child, I assumed that she knew everything. Smart, insightful, poetic, and philosophical, she was always a confidante to others. She once confessed to me that, even as a child, many believed that she had special wisdom and they came to her for advice. We were very close and quite good friends when I was a child and again when I was an adult. But my relationship with her was always tinged with "issues." She had suffered so much. That suffering amazed me, and, in the many ways I compared myself to her, it made me feel like a lesser person. I hoped to be prettier, taller, more fashionable, more American, better educated. But I knew I could never be a better person because I could not suffer as she had. I could not have endured the pain, the separations, the losses, the cold, and the hunger. I could not have endured the humiliation. The suffering was her virtue and my curse. She had suffered, and I was born; she suffered, and, as a result, I was born. She loved me very much, but I could never compensate for her suffering although I did try all my life.

Compensation was what my history was all about. By knowing this history, I compensated for my lack of memory. To know the past, I could open a dimension my mother had inhabited, though not her precise history. To know a different past was to compensate for the terribleness of the past she had lived. Then what happened to the witness she had borne? Witness can only be given to the exact and precise details of particular events. What happened to the witness that destroyed her past and filled my childhood with stories of Lodz? Where does the witnessing go when you adopt a different past?

I lived for more than fifty years in the United States and thirty-five years as a student of history before I could face that question. All my life I knew that I could not bear witness. I had not been there. I had not suffered. I could never know what they knew and could never pretend to know it. But as a historian I had learned to provide something different for that unknowable past. I had learned as a scholar and teacher to make it meaningful by providing some way to connect it with the present—my present and my students' present. I had tried to make history full of the life people had once lived. I had learned to give integrity and meaning to the people whose distinct and particular lives were entombed by the broad strokes of history. This was as much as I could ever do with pasts I had not known and not witnessed. I was a historian.

When I finally took up their history, telling about my parents' past required something more than my profession as a historian. Their past had to become once again my past, a past I was willing to acknowledge and to accept. So I finally went to Poland, to my mother's Poland, frightening and repulsive as it had always been to me, and I brought my daughter, Bluma, named after her grandmother. I brought with me a list of names of children whom I had never known but who had been meaningful to me all my life—including my mother's son Wolf, about whom I had often fantasized as an adolescent. And those names, no more than sacred tokens of their transitory identity, allowed me to find some historical documents and to give these brothers and sisters a place in the book I was going to write about my mother's Poland. I had always made history work for me. Now I prepared to make myself useful to it and to my family.

In writing this memoir, I tried to reconnect with a past I had inherited but set aside—never forgotten—just ignored. I found making the connection difficult at best, not just because the memories had grown thinner. During most of my childhood, I thought I knew too much.

Above all, I knew about their deadly past. And in knowing about this, I felt always apart from others, hardly a child of my time. Now, I know better. No matter how much I can remember, I simply know too little, and there is no one left for me to ask.

In an interview I once claimed that I became a historian because I needed to explore the dark cave of my parents' past. What I must have meant was that the past was always alive for me with mysteries, real presences that required illumination, and to this end I had devoted my career. Standing outside this cave, one gave meaning to those mysteries by investing them with significance. As a historian, I had long believed that this emphasis on the historian's contribution was fundamental. Facts were only facts, but as historians we emphasize context and perspective. Now I know that in trying to reconnect to this most essential history, the facts count the most. Some of these I found in Poland—the streets for which I had names, the shape of ghettos, the fragrance of acacia trees. From documents, I even learned the names of my father's wife and my mother's husband, individuals whose peripheral existence in my childhood were truly important to my parents in their former lives. From the extraordinary archive Jewish Records Indexing—Poland (JRI), I learned to locate (possible) relatives as far back as the early nineteenth century because someone had gathered the records of birth, death, and marriages throughout Poland with the understanding that the names of these real people may be meaningful to others.[1] There are other kinds of facts harder to obtain, but I now value them much more than any schooled perspective: Did my grandmother's

1.   Through this source I found Wolf Nawry (almost certainly my mother's grandfather after whom she named her own son Wolf), as one of several Nawrys born in Warsawa Gubernia (Warsaw Province) in 1859 (twenty years before my grandmother Pola). This birthplace corresponds with my grandmother's birth registration in the Litzmannstadt Ghetto, which locates her birthplace as Wyszogrod, just north of Warsaw. A Prussian connection is tenuous but possible. Thanks to my good friend, Gerry Caspary, I have found a Lewin Nawra (another form of the same name) listed in the compilation by David Luft of *The Naturalized Jews of the Grand Duchy of Posen in 1834 and 1835*, thus showing how the name may have originated there.

family, the Nawrys once move from Prussia to Poland, and if so when and why? Where and how exactly did my uncle live in the deep Russia of which he spoke? When exactly did my father and his family leave the Lodz ghetto (and when did they arrive) after it was shut down and cleared out? Did he go to Auschwitz with all his children or just one or two? Where is my grandfather Moshe buried? What were they like, these paternal grandparents of whom I know so little? Their sad faces in the photo tell me something, but not enough. Where are the Fasses from? I know so little about my father's parents that I am now surprised never to have asked. Was it because I was afraid of that past or afraid of asking my father to remember it? How did my parents get from their liberations to life in Hannover? Why did my father's hands tremble and why did my mother's soul finally break?

A few of these things I may learn when I revisit Poland and exercise my historian's arts on documents (never altogether trustworthy, but especially untrustworthy for Jews), and my learned ability to reason from general historical patterns to specific cases. But nothing will really substitute for the detailed descriptions that my mother could provide or the stories my father and uncle told of life before the catastrophe. I cannot recapture the conversations my parents had with each other that I overheard or that my mother had with my uncle Jerry, or with her American Tante Toby when they animatedly reminded each other of people each had known but who are not known to me even by name. I miss their presence now not just as a child misses a parent, but as a pupil misses a teacher. I need the density of information only they could provide. Hitler succeeded in wiping so much away, both the human and the human traces in trying to bury a whole people; it is by no means easy to reconstruct the lives of the Eastern European Jews in the past, despite the accounts that some ghetto historians managed to hide in cellars in Warsaw and Lodz (where they "witnessed" in the truest sense), despite the wall of photos at the Holocaust museum, although these are an enormous help.

I have told my students often that what matters most is not any particular fact or set of facts, but a relationship to the past, a positioning of the self between the past and the future. And that is surely what I did. Now, I find myself regretting such lessons, not because they are wrong, but because they are blithely optimistic and insufficient. I say these things to not frighten students away from history, which they too often view as nothing more than the deadening detritus of past facts, and to give them a reason to know and own their past. But I had been frightened away from my past also, by its facts, by its load, by its deadliness. In discounting these facts, I denied the value of what we do as historians rather than what is done by movie makers and mythmaking politicians. Facts keep us honest and give us the pleasure (and pain) of detail. They surprise us with their whimsy and force us out of smug cliché. We do not have the right to positions without the facts; we can adopt no perspectives in their absence. We retrieve facts from the past because we need to know them, because they are our nearest borrowing from truth.

I have always felt a special affinity for the novels of Saul Bellow (despite their misogyny). Now I think I know why. I was drawn to his rich language and fact-stuffed descriptions of people, especially, but also of things like clothes and American places, all made tangible through a tactile language of detail. These stories of American Jews I found infinitely fascinating; they were somehow people I needed to know better, and Bellow made this possible. Bellow provided me with Jewish characters very unlike those I grew up among, but which I might have known had my grandfather stayed in America instead of returning to Poland. My mother had a similar love for the stories of Isaac Bashevis Singer, all those tales she read and savored, despite his mystical cover, the *narishkeit* (nonsense) as she called it. She loved the details of place and personality, mostly of Poland, Polish Jews, and of Polish Jews out of place in America. She was drawn to the particulars of a life lived with color and the sound of language spoken. She loved the specificity of character. She had found her Jewish author, and I had found mine.

Now I need to know more, much more about the very specific past from which my consciousness (no longer divided, but still scarred) has grown. This means knowing not only about the Shoah, but about the long history before that. Despite my studies of the past, I had long shunned Jewish history because it forced my attachment. Now that this attachment is freely given, this history has become a necessity to me, and I have only begun to explore it as I sought out a context for the people in this book. These readings in Jewish history can now people my past with nineteenth-century Galician innkeepers and eighteenth-century Prussian dealers in grain, a host of Hasidim, but just as many Maskilim, and all those strong women.

Some things I do not need to know nor do I want to know more about: How did it feel to leave a three-year-old (already terribly undernourished and cold) with thousands of other children whose fate was certain? How did one fail to say goodbye to a mother at the gate to hell? The imagination is enough. Such intimacies of feeling are best left to themselves. And I do not want to know the process of their deaths, which have become a modern obsession. In having such dominion over our memory of the Jewish past by meting out death to the people and the culture, the Holocaust has shuttered out the significant facts of life. In retrieving that life, we deny to the Nazi death machine its ultimate purpose. I want to know facts about the life of a young woman alive and dreaming in Poland during the 1920s, of children born and alive in the 1930s, of shopping on the *ul* Piotrkowska (that my mother always called Pietakowa), and working in the Lodz ghetto before the war. Rude abstractions do not cover these bases, nor does the sadistic logic of a Nazi-commissioned fate.

When I was a child, I thought as a child (almost) and wanted some space to grow between the edges of the stories my parents told of a life once lived in a past now gone. As a grownup, I want to pass some of this along to my children who will have to find their own spaces to grow in.

AFTERWORD

POLAND, AGAIN

I knew I would return, if only because there was so much more to understand. But when I did return with my husband, Jack, in the summer of 2007, Lodz had changed. Its aura as a city caught in amber, a fossilized kernel of my parents' past, had largely disappeared. *Ul* Piotrkowska was still there, as were the old houses and streets, but like many other parts of Poland, the city had moved beyond the postwar (and with it the prewar) into a new era. Part of the Lodz and Poland I had found seven years earlier was surely the romantic haze I brought to the experience, and that haze was gone with familiarity. It was familiar to me now, not as the source of my mother's stories, but as a site I had explored as a tourist. There were no more wonderful discoveries in turning the corner of a street or looking into a dark courtyard. That sense of experience and memories merging into a dreamlike reality was gone. I could now show Jack around, as an insider, knowledgeable and harder to impress. I was also in contact with my earlier hosts who had become friends. Lodz, now a city I knew, not the unknown city of my childhood, had been transformed. But the change was not just in me and the repetition of experience. The city had changed, and the divide between my father's Lodz and my mother's Lodz had virtually disappeared.

Poznanski's factory—the source of his fabled Jewish wealth—which had marked the middle ground, the place where the city divided into two, had been remade. In place of a somber dark brick factory with hundreds of workers, stood the "Manufactura," an elaborate shopping mall, housed in the cleaned-up hull of the former plant, and now the site of Lodz's claim to fame. The city that had produced textiles by the mile was adapting to its post-EU life, moving with the rest of the West, from production to consumption. The Poland I had known from my mother's stories was backward and grey; I had found this Poland in its postcommunist incarnation in May 2000, no longer deeply backward by Western standards, but still far behind places in Western Europe or the United States. That was no longer true. Where a city had once been carved into the countryside in the nineteenth century to help clothe Russia and the East, there was now an enormous mall that conveyed through its shops, restaurants, and movie theatres the goods, tastes, and style of the West. Famous brands, like Guess and Polo, had their outlets here cheek-by-jowl with Lodz's own historical shop brands such as Kruik jewelers or Rylko shoes. The restaurants all had foreign food menus, from Italian to American fast food. Beyond the consumption of goods, Lodz was now making strides in manufacturing pseudo-experience. Indeed, at the center of the "Manufactura" we found a huge sanded area with plastic palm trees and thatched huts, meant to evoke Hawaii. This was a city very distant from the Lodz that my mother had known and which I had both yearned to understand and feared as a child.

Today Lodz is a city that looks to the future by accepting as part of its past four groups with which it identifies and for which it now hosts yearly cultural festivals. Remembering its once heterogeneous population, and embracing the differences which were once a troubling part of its nationhood, Lodz enshrines Polish, Jewish, German, and Russian cultures as part of its heritage, a tribute to its complex past and a means to allow these people to feel comfortable returning as tourists and shoppers. On our first day in Lodz, our hosts took us to a "Jewish Restaurant" called Anatewka (in recollection of Shalom Aleichem's Tevia the Milkman, but really to its modern *Fiddler on the Roof* incarnation). Here, just off *ul* Piotrkowka, in what was once my mother's part of the city, a Polish restaurateur serves variants on Jewish food while a young female dressed in Hasidic boy's garb sits on an indoor roof made of thatch and plays old Jewish airs. I was not happy but could not insult our kind and well-meaning hosts by saying so.

The food was barely Jewish and certainly not kosher, and the chopped veal in a cream sauce was in fact a contradiction of the very idea of a Jewish kitchen. The various portraits, in oils, of old Hasidim (really someone's idea of Hasidim) made me reel. This was how my relatives had now been absorbed—as graven images—into the décor. The very idea of these people as part of a style seemed obscene. My dead ancestors had become a motif for modern amusement. Everything about the restaurant was wrong, from the matzos mixed into the bread basket (just the kind of sinful juxtaposition that would have made my mother despair), to the little figures (about an inch high) of Hasidim in *talits* we were given as parting presents. Here were Jewish figures literally turned into consumer idols. I never went back.

This reabsorption of its past is now the reality in Poland. It has not only allowed the Poles to move forward into the twenty-first-century economy (and who can blame them?) but also backward into an alliance with a history over which they had never really been in full control. Poland was in fact a product of Poles, Jews, Germans, and Russians, though in the past Polish nationalists had chafed at this dependence. Now it was a heritage. When I visited in 2000, I sensed that, whatever their ambivalence, the Poles actually missed the Jews. They knew that they suffered from their absence in the professions, the arts, and in economic activity. Poland itself was in many ways incomplete without them. This is no longer true. Lodz and Poland have moved strongly forward, embracing their opportunities without needing Jews as they once did, except as myths. Where they once needed real Jews, they now include dead Jews in their new commercial world.

My father's Lodz was the best illustration of Poland's comfortable adjustment to a world without Jews. Jack and I went to the old ghetto area, a ghetto even before the Nazis came. Many of the old buildings had finally been taken down, while others had been renovated. There were workers and rubble in pockets throughout the area. (My father's diamonds were surely discovered by now.) The hovels and outhouses, the decayed apartments and the broken streets that I had still recognized as my father's old childhood haunts, were mostly gone. The usable buildings, especially on main arteries such as Zgierska, had been refurbished and now contained nice shops. Indeed, most of the bridal shops that I had seen on Piotrkowska during my first visit to Lodz, seemed to have moved into this former Jewish ghetto. And the old market (known as the new market) was lush. Fresh fruits and vegetables in abundance, breads and cookies, new socks and shirts were laid out in profusion. The market, many of its stalls covered in awning, was now designated as a bazaar by my host and signaled Lodz's prosperity. The sharp divide between the prestigious (non-Jewish) Lodz and the ramshackle Jewish ghetto (including the worst part of this ghetto surrounding the market, formerly known as Balut) was gone. They were bridged by the new-old, but certainly modern Manufactura.

Why should the old ghetto remain? What was the Polish investment in keeping it alive? The reason for the divide—the need to house the many alien Jews—was gone. All that was identifiably left of the Nazi encampment, what had been the Litzmannstadt ghetto, was the brown wooden building where the punishing interrogations by the Gestapo had taken place, under German auspices, and the façade of the hospital. In this building my uncle Avrum had probably worked and gained some of the knowledge that permitted my mother's family (but not her three-year-old son) to survive the years of disease, starvation, and selection. It was not clear whether even this hulk of a past life and death would survive the modern selection of city buildings. In the end, I expect the only building that will be preserved will be the structure where the interrogations took place—the chosen object of historical memory now surrounded by a protective wire fence. To their considerable credit, the

Poles and the remaining Jews of the city had enshrined the terrible train station, Radogoszcz, as a memorial to the hundreds of thousands of Jews who had been herded toward their death by cattle car to the many extermination camps of the German Reich. One of the cattle cars is still there. I would have missed the Radogoszcz if my thoughtful and historically alert hosts had not taken me to this place of terrible remembrance.

Not only was the ghetto gone because the Jews were now long gone, but the process of historical recording was replacing the life of a people with various forms of commemoration, some more historically effective than others. In Warsaw, for example, in the green across from the memorial to the Warsaw uprising, Jack and I entered a white tent marking the beginnings of a major new museum that hoped to collect and exhibit materials about the life of the Jews in Poland during the many hundreds of years of their residence there. While still in embryo, this project has it right in seeking to understand and teach about the long life and significant place of Jewish culture in Polish history and of the Jews as a fundamental constituent of whatever it meant to be Poland for most of its history. At least, it might some day become such a memorial. This was a far cry from the Anatewka Restaurant. In the Isaak Synagogue in Krakow, however, the exhibition I had seen on Jewish life in Galicia in the early twentieth century had disappeared. Instead, the synagogue was being completely cleaned up, repainted, and renovated as a tourist magnet—one of the several edifices that now serve as part of what has become the Jewish Museum of Krakow. Prettified and emptied of its exhibit of poor Jews with their dilapidated houses and louse-ridden children, the Isaak Synagogue could now represent what modern Poles (and modern Jews too, for that matter) would like to remember as part of their heritage—a graceful, clean old building with decorative Hebrew lettering on the walls and simple wooden pews. Krakow's ghetto, too, is gone. I was repeatedly met by empty stares when I asked people to direct me to the ghetto area. No one seemed to know what I was talking about until I asked for Schindler's factory (known as a result of the movie). Only then was I offered directions. The Galicia to which Western European Jews sent charity is no longer part of the history told here as Western Europe and the former Eastern Europe merge into a modern European Union.

Daniel Mendelsohn, whose own inquiries and odyssey into his family's fate can be read in the brilliant *The Lost*, told Teri Gross on National Public Radio that all of Eastern Europe feels empty, missing an essential component of its society in the absence of its Jews. Well, maybe that is how it felt to him as he sought the missing part of his family. In fact, however, Poles do not seem to be missing the Jews at all, but rapidly substituting myths and monuments for the people and their complex cultural expressions. These people had once been an intimate part of Poznanski's brick factory as well as his baroque palace, they had gathered to pray at the orthodox Krakower synagogue, and lived in the poor ghetto quarters in Lodz and elsewhere where large families held on to a very bare existence. The Poles are not missing the problems caused by these stubborn, strong-willed people (called stiff necked for their failure to bow down to Christ), whose lives were marked by their own rituals, their own calendar, and their own language as well as their own religious observances. These observances from birth through death were beautifully described in the exhibit in Krakow's oldest synagogue, much as one would describe the rituals of Roman pagans or Native Americans. The Jews were hard to live with. It is easier to remember them fondly in festivals, museums, and empty synagogues. Today I am afraid they are not being missed at all either in Poland or by Poles. More frightening, their absence is increasingly not felt because other things have been substituted for it, and the Poles have absorbed the substitutions into their own history. Thus tourists will come to believe this to be "the history of the Jews in Poland."

I know another history. My memories may be only memories of memories (secondhand goods like the kind once sold in the market in Lodz), but they whisper to me of another life lived in Poland than the one that is being reconstructed in the Poland to which I recently returned. For the first time, I tried to seek out the scents of an older Jewish life in Torùn and Lask. These are places that most heritage tourists ignore. I decided that I would try to look beneath and before Lodz. I had learned that my grandmother's unusual maiden name, Nawry, indicated an origin in the Prussia near the old Hanseatic town of Torùn, with its fabled Teutonic knights. Maybe the rain and cold in mid-July kept me off the scent, but when Jack and I visited Torùn, we found lots of early remnants of the gothic city and of Nicholas Copernicus, its most famous native son and a great Polish hero, but no sign of Nawrys or other Jews. Torùn's museum in its ancient town hall gave elaborate evidence of centuries of Christian worship and the skilled handicrafts of guilds that supervised beautiful work in locks, tiles, and other crafts. But there were no displays that spoke of the merchants, large and small, among whom the Jews were most likely to be found. This omission was serious in a town whose favored location on the Vistula connected it to the rich traffic of the Baltic Sea. Today Torùn trades on its famous gingerbread and wooden children's toys and various other knick-knacks. But the people who once supplied the country's basic needs and connected its rich hinterland of grain to the rest of Poland and distant European ports are forgotten, or at least not anywhere on display.

And we visited Lask, an old market town, about half an hour's car trip from Lodz, because my grandfather Israel Sieradzki was born there. Much older than Lodz, Lask was founded in the fifteenth century, even before Columbus came to the new world. Poor and provincial, Lask still contains houses that look like they are little more than shelters from the elements. I looked into the open door of one of these and saw bare earthen walls and very low ceilings, still poor and still inhabited. This Lask was not yet part of new EU Poland. I found two items of note here: a huge old water pump in the town square, beautifully embellished and sturdy, and an enormous Catholic Church. (Had my grandfather mistakenly walked near this church at Easter time and been pummeled for being a Jew?) No sign of Jews or the remembrance of Jews marred the historical reality that still lay on the face of Lask, though like most small

towns in the province of Lodz and throughout Poland, it had once been
home to many Jews. Indeed, Jews had lived in Lask for four hundred
years. Ten minutes further by automobile, we arrived at Zdunska Wola,
once a beautiful resort town, full of members of my extended family.
It had been a point of pride to live here because it was a cultured place,
with an enormous, elegant park, as my mother had told me. It too was
very run down, but unlike Lask, Zdunska Wola was clearly beginning to
recover its former polish as workers painted formerly elaborate facades
in fanciful colors, just as they were doing in Lodz. Here we ate lunch in
an enormous, almost empty, elaborately overdecorated restaurant/hotel/
night club, called of all things "Hades," which also sought to recall the
city's former aura of elegance. These places, just too far off the beaten
track for tourists and heritage seekers, are still full of history. But unlike
places such as Lodz and Krakow that now celebrate their Jewish remains,
there is no evidence that real Jews are missed or missing here. There are
not even ersatz remains. The Poles even in these places have adapted
quite well to the absence of Jews; indeed, they are hardly even absent.

I decided that this would be my last trip to Poland. It may no longer
be a place I am ashamed of, but it is very far away from California. Its
distance in space now substitutes in discomfort for its former historical
distance. It is an inconvenient place to visit. I was glad that I had come
when it was just discovering itself after the end of communism. Less
glad to have come this second time, I still felt that as a historian, seeing
the way Poland was responding to its present and representing its past
was important to observe. I had no interest in watching this process any
further erode my memories or what I knew about my family. My history would have to subsist on what I already knew about the place from
which they had come and what I, as a historian, could still imagine. I was
unlikely to find much more as Poland rapidly evolved into a future in
which my family's past would have no place. The German-Yiddish word
Zukunft (future) haunts me as I realize that there is no future in Poland
for the Jews I have known either in person or in my mother and father's

stories. There may also be no real *Verganginheit* (past) in that Poland. As memoirist/historian, I will have to salvage what I can of that past.

I will probably not return to Poland, but I have decided to leave a small piece of my memories behind in the Jewish cemetery in Lodz. This peaceful, even beautiful place, Jack agreed, was worthy of remembrance. To this end, I am having a plaque commemorating my family placed on the wall inside the cemetery. It reads:

In memory of the members of my family who lived in Lodz and died here and throughout Poland during the Nazi occupation of Europe in World War II.

Paula Fass

My grandparents:
Moshe Aron Fass and Scheindel Felzner Fass
Israel Favel Sieradzki and Pola Nawry Sieradzki

My sisters and brothers:
Wolf Leib Kromolowski
Branja Fass
Henja Malka Fass
Szabsaj David Fass
Abraham Isaak Fass

My uncles, aunts, and cousins:
Abram Sieradzki
Chana Sieradzka
Rozia Fass
Abram Szmul Fass

And many, many others including:
Zaynwel Kopel Kromolowski
Alta Izbicka Fass

APPENDIX

FAMILY TREE

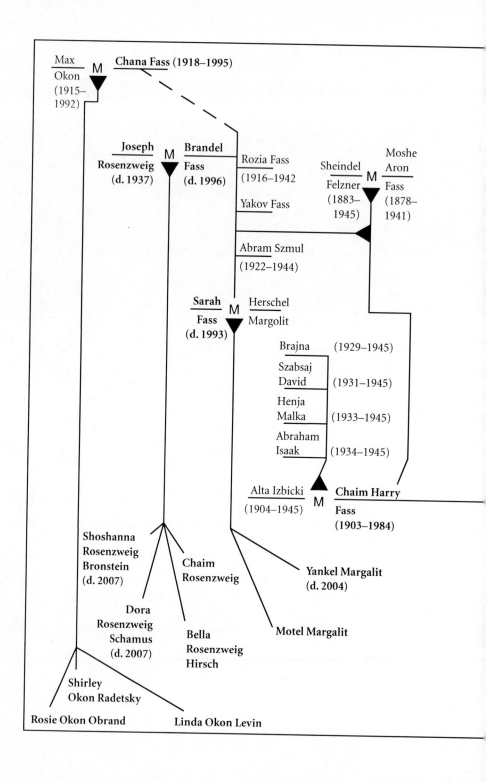

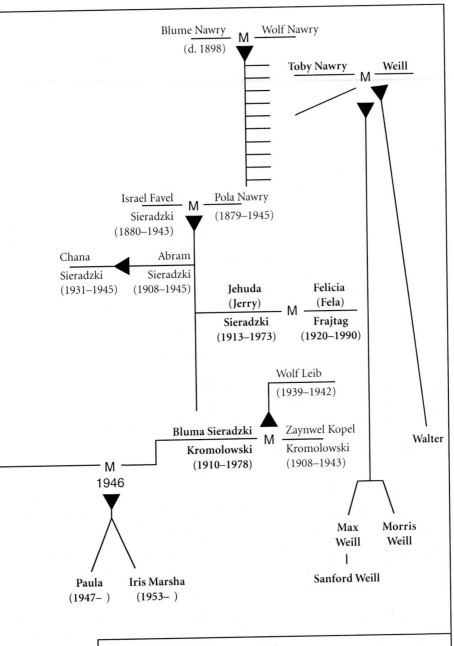

Blume Nawry
(d. 1898)   **M**   Wolf Nawry

Toby Nawry   **M**   **Weill**

Israel Favel   **M**   Pola Nawry
Sieradzki   (1879–1945)
(1880–1943)

Chana   Abram
Sieradzki   Sieradzki
(1931–1945)   (1908–1945)

Jehuda   **Felicia**
(Jerry)   **(Fela)**
M
Sieradzki   **Frajtag**
(1913–1973) **(1920–1990)**

Wolf Leib
(1939–1942)

Bluma Sieradzki   Zaynwel Kopel
Kromolowski   **M**   Kromolowski
(1910–1978)   (1908–1943)

M
1946   **Walter**

Paula   **Iris Marsha**
(1947–)   **(1953–)**

Max   **Morris**
Weill   **Weill**

Sanford Weill

NOTE:
Persons who survived or were born after the war are shown in boldface.
Persons who did not survive the war are shown in roman.

ABOUT THE AUTHOR

PAULA S. FASS, the Margaret Byrne Professor of History at the University of California at Berkeley, specializes in the social and cultural history of the United States. Before going to Berkeley in 1974, she taught at Rutgers University. Her books include *The Damned and the Beautiful: American Youth in the 1920s* (1977), *Outside In: Minorities and the Transformation of American Education* (1989), *Kidnapped: Child Abduction in the United States* (1997), and *Children of a New World: Society, Culture, and Globalization* (2007). She is the editor of *Childhood in America* (2000) and the three-volume *Encyclopedia of Children and Childhood in History and Society* (2004). She currently serves as the president of the Society for the History of Children and Youth. Paula Fass lives in Berkeley, California, with her husband John Lesch.